Price Waterhouse is a leading worldwide professional organization of tax practitioners, auditors, and management consultants. Operating from over 400 offices in more than 100 countries and territories, Price Waterhouse firms provide a variety of services to businesses, individuals, government entities, and nonprofit organizations.

The Price Waterhouse U.S. firm frequently consults with the Treasury Department and the Internal Revenue Service on tax issues. The firm also offers seminars and publishes a variety of periodicals and booklets on tax and personal financial planning subjects.

Through its more than 100 U.S. offices and its legislative monitoring service in Washington, D.C., Price Waterhouse advises businesses and individuals nationwide on the planning and compliance implications of the tax law.

THE PRICE WATERHOUSE RETIREMENT PLANNING ADVISER

1990-1991 EDITION

New York London Toronto Sydney Tokyo Singapore

This publication contains information on the tax law as of August 17, 1990, and does not reflect developments since that date. Such developments could include amendments to the Internal Revenue Code, promulgation of new tax regulations, other actions and interpretations by the Internal Revenue Service, and court decisions relating to the law. This publication is intended to offer information on personal tax matters to individuals who are cash basis taxpayers. It is sold with the understanding that the author and publisher are not herein engaged in rendering legal, tax, or other professional services. This book should not be used as a substitute for personal consultations with professional tax advisers.

POCKET BOOKS, a division of Simon &
Schuster, Inc. 1230 Avenue of the Americas,
New York, N.Y. 10020.

ISBN: 0-671-72880-6

First Pocket Books printing October, 1990

10 9 8 7 6 5 4 3 2 1

Printed in the U.S.A.

Contents

As We Went To Press . . .

Congress and the Administration were discussing various options to be included in a deficit reduction package. Although no one can say for certain what the final outcome will be, the chances of reaching an agreement were greatly increased after President Bush stated that tax revenue increases would be a necessary part of the deficit reduction package. Most of the ideas have been put forth as a way of raising additional revenue because of the substantial pressure to meet deficit reduction targets for 1991, although a few of them may provide for or extend certain tax breaks.

Since a number of these proposals could impact your retirement planning, we thought it would be helpful to summarize some of the major items.

- **Capital gains tax reduction.** At present, capital gains (long term) and ordinary income are taxed at the same rate. President Bush has been a proponent of lowering the capital gains tax rate for individuals to encourage capital investment. However, it appears that if such a tax reduction is implemented, it may be accompanied by an individual marginal tax rate increase.

  ☞ CAUTION At this time, neither the effective date of any reduction in the capital gains tax rate, nor the form such a reduction might take, is known. You should make sure that, if such a reduction in rates is passed and you attempt to take advantage of the reduction, your sale of a capital asset falls within the effective dates for a lower capital gains tax.

- **Stocks and bonds excise tax.** To raise revenue, an excise tax on the purchase or sale of stocks and bonds is being considered. This could lower the net proceeds received from the sale of securities or increase the cost to purchase such securities.

- **Other excise taxes.** To raise additional revenue, further excise taxes are being considered including a new broad based energy tax, an increase in alcohol and tobacco excise taxes, and an extension of the expiring 3% telephone excise tax. Any or all of these or other excise taxes may be included in a deficit reduction package.
- **Expiring tax provisions.** Certain tax provisions are currently set to expire in the near future. These include the deduction of 25% of health insurance premiums paid by self-employed persons and the exclusion from employee's income of certain tuition reimbursements made by employers. Due to the broad based support for these items, they may be further extended.
- **Tax deferred savings.** There has been a push to reinstate a tax-driven savings plan. This plan would give preferential tax treatment to investment in and/or accumulation of earnings in a savings account. The treatment may be similar to an individual retirement account. The Bush Administration's version of this proposal is called a family savings account.

There are a great number of other options currently included in the deficit reduction discussions. Included in these are limitations on state and local tax deductions and further limitations on interest expense deductions.

However, keep in mind that, if they are enacted into law, they may affect your tax retirement planning. As a result, you should consult with your tax adviser to determine how any of the proposals may affect you.

Introduction

The years that you spend in retirement can be among the best of your life. They can bring you the freedom and opportunity to engage in activities for which you've never had time, to start another career, to work in public service, to travel—to do whatever you like. But this view of retirement as a time for growth and exploration is a new one.

In the 1940s and into the 1950s, when people anticipated retirement it was almost the same as planning for death. The actuarial life expectancy in the 1940s was roughly age sixty-nine. Long-term retirement planning consisted of picking a burial plot.

For those who did live beyond their work years, the financial aspects of retirement were typically simple. They often had few assets relying instead on a steady income from a company pension plan and from Social Security. If the income wasn't much, it was at least regular, and all they had to do to get it was walk to the mailbox.

Old perceptions die hard. Retirement isn't at all the

same as it used to be. And the financial aspects of retirement certainly aren't as simple for several reasons:

- Retirees today can expect to live for another 20 or more years. Retirement is no longer a short rest on the porch swing.
- Most future retirees won't get regular checks in the mail from company pension plans, but monthly statements from brokers or financial managers reporting on the performance of their investment portfolios.
- Social Security is no longer large enough to cover most of your basic post-retirement expenses.
- Steady inflation, which wasn't a factor 40 years ago, today eats away at the purchasing power of even a comfortable retirement income.
- Finally, retirees today simply want more than their parents or grandparents did.

When Great-grandpa thought about retirement, there was just one question he could ask: How big is the check going to be? He had very little opportunity to be involved in planning for his and Great-grandma's later years. That's not so for working people today.

Even those just starting their careers must decide when they need to start saving in order to finance the lengthy retirement they can anticipate. Once they've started putting money aside, they have to be concerned with investing it. And then, on retirement, even more issues arise. How do you start drawing money out of your various investment plans? What's the best tax strategy? How do you alter your investment strategy to insure reasonable liquidity and income while protecting principal? What must you do to preserve the purchasing power of your income in the face of inflation?

Planning for retirement doesn't have to be worrisome or unpleasant. It doesn't have to take a lot of time, and you don't need to be a financial genius. What you do need is interest, some basic knowledge, and the good sense not to make mistakes that you can easily avoid.

We've written a book that we hope will pique your interest. We know that it incorporates all the essential information you'll need to create or revamp your financial retirement plan. And, we've tried to call attention to the mistakes people commonly make.

Our approach is simple and straightforward. We'll help you figure out where you stand financially now with respect to retirement. We'll help you figure out where you want to be. Then, naturally, we'll help you create the strategies that will take you there.

But let's not forget that there's more to retirement planning that assuring yourself of an adequate income.

What are you going to do with this money? With your time? How is your day going to change? Remember, you may be retired for as long as you have been working. Will your colleagues at the office be your lifelong friends? The relationships you have with your family probably won't be the same. And what about those health issues you've avoided thinking much about? Smoking? The extra couple of pounds you've been adding every year? They'll matter more over the next thirty years than over the past.

Chapter 2 of this book will help you recognize some of the nonfinancial issues that arise in retirement. Of course, in a book that is primarily about financial planning, we can hope only to remind you that there are other, nonfinancial questions that all of us need to address.

As you read our book, we hope that it motivates you to apply the principles that it outlines to your own life planning. We hope that it encourages you to think positively about the enormous potential you have to influence the shape and the quality of your retirement years.

Right now you are building the ship that will carry you through the rest of your life. Read on, and good sailing.

1

Understanding Today's Reality

There may be fundamental truths on which you can always rely—but not in retirement planning. Retirement plans that you don't periodically reexamine and revise in the light of altered conditions can be worse than no plans at all. If you have no plan, at least you know it, but a plan based on assumptions that are no longer valid can lull you into false security. And they can be misleading: You *think* you have your situation covered, but you don't. By the time your error becomes apparent, it may be too late to correct it.

Retirement planning, we're sorry to say, is plagued by more than its share of myths and obsolete assumptions—the most dangerous of which we spell out in the pages that follow.

Although some of these assumptions may once have

been true, economic, demographic, and/or social changes have caused them to become outmoded. Here are some of the most commonly encountered myths and misconceptions that you want to be sure to steer clear of:

OLD REALITY: If you're like most people, you only have to save for 10 to 15 years of retirement.

NEW REALITY: If you make it to retirement, you'll probably live to be close to 90. That's almost thirty years of living without a salary income.

The average life span is currently around 75 years, but that fact can play a statistical trick on your retirement planning. The average, you see, also includes the 21 percent of the population that dies before reaching age 65.

In reality, many men who live to 65 will probably see eighty-four. Women who survive to retirement age will likely live to be eighty-eight. To be safe—that is, to be sure that you don't outlive your means—almost everyone today should make financial plans to get themselves through age ninety. We'll spend nearly a third of our lives in retirement.

OLD REALITY: Retirement means getting a good rocker on the porch and watching the world go by.

NEW REALITY: You'll probably be retired a long time before you start slowing down.

Longer retirements mean that you can no longer talk about those years as if they were all the same. Rather, you should think of two phases.

In the early phase you'll hardly be less active than you were when you were working. Maybe you'll be more so. You'll have more time for golf, travel, and other recreation. Your need for disposable income may not decline much at all.

Finally, in the second phase of retirement, you'll begin to slow down. Maybe then you'll put that rocker on the porch. And it's then that you'll have to be prepared to deal with the infirmities of aging and the expenses that they entail.

OLD REALITY: Once you've retired, your financial strategy should aim at preserving your capital.

NEW REALITY: Retirement doesn't mean that you should stop earning and give up saving—not if you expect to beat inflation.

Unless you can expect to be extremely wealthy upon retirement—or you're one of those rare individuals with a pension that's adjusted for inflation—you're going to be more concerned with preserving your spending power over a long retirement period than in preserving capital. Let's say you retire with $500,000 in financial assets at age fifty-five. At an 8 percent annual yield, that principal will give you an income of $40,000 a year. Good enough, you say?

Don't forget inflation. If it creeps along at just 4.5 percent, in ten years your $40,000 income will have only $26,000 in purchasing power; in twenty years, just $17,000; and after thirty years you'll be trying to live on income worth just $11,000.

To keep from getting caught short, you need to continue building your assets during the early post-retirement years. You can continue to work; you can work part-time; or you can aim your investment strategy toward generating higher asset growth.

By working, though, you want to be sure that you don't reduce the Social Security benefits that you receive at that time. And with a high-growth investment strategy, you need to be careful not to expose your capital to greater risk than you are comfortable with.

If you start out with $500,000 and manage to put away an additional $20,000 per year for the first ten years of your retirement either from working or from your high-growth investment strategy, then you'll probably stay well ahead of the inflation curve.

OLD REALITY: In retirement, you'll shell out a smaller percentage of your income for taxes.

NEW REALITY: True, retirement may drop you into a lower tax bracket, but your effective tax rate may not decline at all.

That means that the percentage of your total income that winds up as taxes may not be any less than it was when you were working.

True, marginal federal income tax rates (or the rates charged in each tax bracket) declined as a result of tax reform in 1986. But effective tax rates—the total amount of tax you pay as a percentage of your income—have been going up since Congress enacted the income tax in 1913. That's because the value of exemptions and deductions has declined and because state and local taxes, along with Social Security taxes, have been going up.

Furthermore, future retirees are very likely to pay tax on more and more of the Social Security benefits they receive.

OLD REALITY: You won't need anything more than Social Security to cover your post-retirement basic living costs.

NEW REALITY: Unless you're prepared to live *very*

simply, Social Security will just barely begin to cover your basic post-retirement expenses.

Traditionally, retirees have depended upon Social Security to cover their basic post-retirement expenses, but not anymore. People do want their lifestyles to change after retirement—but for the better. That means many of their expenses won't go down. In fact, some may even go up. So retirees have to look beyond Social Security for the income they need to provide them with the lifestyle they desire.

OLD REALITY: You'll be able to use the defined-benefit pension from your employer as your principle source of income during your retirement years.

NEW REALITY: Your employer may not even offer a defined-benefit pension plan.

Traditionally, retirees have depended upon their former employers' defined-benefit pension plans to provide their retirement incomes. Defined-benefit plans paid each retiree a fixed income, although it usually wasn't adjusted for inflation.

The size of the pension you drew depended largely on your years of service and your compensation while you were employed. Whatever the pension was, though, every month a check for that amount arrived in the mail. It was as simple as that.

That's because the people running the company retirement plan made all the investment decisions. If they made a mistake, the company was obliged to make good. Except for cashing the check, you didn't have to be involved.

Many large employers still have defined-benefit retirement plans, but the number is dwindling. And the number of smaller companies and younger companies that offer employees these kinds of plans is close to nil. Instead, businesses are providing defined-contribution plans. For potential retirees, the differences are significant.

Defined-contribution plans include those based on profit sharing, 401(k) savings, and employee stock ownership. More than three-quarters of all new retirement plans created since 1974 fall into this defined-contribution category.

With-defined contribution plans, you don't know how much you'll receive on retirement. Your employer's obligation is only to make a specified contribution to the plan—or to allow you to make it. With a 401(k) savings plan, for instance, the entire contribution may come from you. With a profit sharing plan, if there are no profits the specified contribution may be zero.

Furthermore, with defined-contribution plans you may have some responsibility to make decisions about how the funds in your account are invested as they build up before retirement. And when you do retire, the entire job of managing a lump-sum payout from the company may fall to you.

In other words, defined-contribution plans require you to play a much more active role in managing your money both before and after retirement. But with that control comes a great deal more uncertainty. If your money is invested in stocks and the stock market crashes the month before you retire, it isn't the plan's problem but yours.

OLD REALITY: Job hopping or chasing higher salaries doesn't make sense. If you stick with one company for your whole career, it will pay off in a richer retirement.

NEW REALITY: Staying in the wrong job for the right pension doesn't even make good economic sense, let alone good professional or business sense any more.

It's pointless to be miserable in a job you don't like just to capture the pension benefits, because often you will end up costing yourself money in the long run. Here's why. Defined-benefit pension plans typically pay off at a rate tied to your highest pay while at the company— whether you were there for ten years or forty. So if you stay with a job that pays less than you could get by switching, you may actually be reducing the size of your pension check.

Of course, with defined-benefit plans you must stay with the company long enough to become vested in the plan. You should know the vesting period before you make the jump. Sometimes a short delay in shifting jobs will be worth the wait.

With defined-contribution plans, especially the employee-funded variety such as 401(k) plans, your plan travels with you when you switch jobs. You need only stay long enough to be vested in the employer-matching contribution. Then, if you can do better, move on.

OLD REALITY: Your income will rise, and you'll be able to put more money away for retirement in the latter stages of your career.

NEW REALITY: Don't count on it.

Lot's of today's two-income households put off having children until they were closing in on forty. Consequently, they're going to reach retirement age at about the same time that their children's education expenses are the highest. There goes the money they would have stashed away for their imminent retirement.

OLD REALITY: When people started work right after college, kept at it until they retired at age sixty-five, and then lived another five or ten years into retirement, there was plenty of time to save.

NEW REALITY: With earlier retirement and longer retirement periods, there's less time available to save for the nest egg you want.

To begin with, you need to save more. Furthermore, you have less time in which to do it. The compounding of interest or other investment earnings will work wonders on even relatively small amounts of capital over time—but it does take time.

Say you'll need $200,000 for your retirement nest egg. And you can earn an 8 percent rate of return each year. Say, too, you'll need this amount by age sixty. If you're forty years old and plan to retire when you're sixty, you'll need to save $4,400 a year for the next 20 years. If you're forty-five, you'll need to save $7,400 a year for 15 years. If you're fifty, you'll need to save $13,800 a year for 10 years. If you're fifty-five, a mere five years from retirement, you'll need to save a whopping $34,100 a year for 5 years. What if you can't alter your present lifestyle to save that much? Then you'll have to alter your retirement lifestyle.

OLD REALITY: Your housing costs will plummet.

NEW REALITY: Your property taxes are likely to go up along with your maintenance costs.

It's nice that your mortgage might be paid off, but if you've been paying it for thirty years, inflation has reduced its real cost anyway. What hasn't gone down is any other housing-related expense: maintenance, taxes, or energy. Statistics show that older people pay a greater portion of their income for housing than younger people—31 percent for the older-than-sixty-five crowd versus 27 percent for those between forty-five and sixty-five.

You can cut your housing costs in any number of ways—renting a smaller apartment, for instance. Or you can increase your income by renting a portion of your home to, for instance, a student or an older person who no longer wishes to live alone. Just don't assume that your housing costs are automatically going to decline.

OLD REALITY: Your responsibilities for other family members will end when you retire.

NEW REALITY: You may have to help support two generations—the one preceding and the one following you.

In increasing numbers, adult children are returning home to live with their parents after finishing college. Twice as many do now as in 1975. Of course, you can always ask them to chip in for the food and household expenses, even to pay rent.

You may not be able to get the same help from the other generation, your parents, who are increasingly likely to move in with you. Sixty percent of the elderly, or thereabouts, are dependent upon their children for housing and/or at least partial support. Even if your aging parents don't live with you, they may depend on your financial help.

Naturally, it's the older elderly—those over eighty-five, say—who need the most help. In twenty years, when baby boomers begin to retire, the number of people older than eighty-five—their parents—will have doubled to 6.6 million.

OLD REALITY: Health insurance should prove no

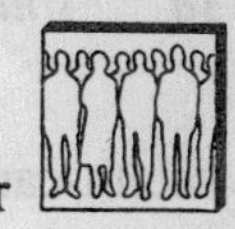

problem. Medicare will take up where your company's basic insurance leaves off.

NEW REALITY: You'd better watch your health, set aside a reserve to pay for increasingly costly insurance, and look for medical cost savings.

Even the largest and most profitable corporations aren't going to continue paying for retirees' health care insurance, and the reason is simple. With health care costs rising at close to 20 percent per year, that means that they will double every three and a half years. No company can afford to keep that up for long.

If that weren't reason enough to discourage continued corporate generosity to retirees, a proposed change in accounting guidelines will require companies, starting in 1993, to record these future obligations to pay health care premiums as an expense on current income statements. This change will reduce reported earnings, which could depress the price of the company's stock.

So, there's a good chance that people retiring soon can expect to see their health insurance premiums rise and their former employer's contribution drop. And if you're a long way from retirement now, you shouldn't count on much help once you leave the work force.

Medicare, by the way, typically covers only half your

health-care expenses, and then not until you reach age sixty-five no matter when you retire.

OLD REALITY: As real estate values continued to climb in almost every part of the country, retirees could count on their homes to provide a substantial asset that they could turn into cash and invest in order to generate income.

NEW REALITY: In Houston, Phoenix, Boston, and even New York, where people swore it could never happen, housing values have stopped growing. Retirees can no longer count on their homes as a ready source of cash when they need it.

The house you buy today could conceivably be worth less than you paid for it when you're ready to retire. And even if the value hasn't depreciated, the dramatic growth that once made us all feel like canny real estate investors has probably disappeared for the foreseeable future. Consequently, it's no longer a good idea to rely on anticipated appreciation of housing values to build your retirement assets. Obviously, we don't know what's going to happen to housing prices, but their continuing escalation is no longer a sure bet.

Ridding yourself of misleading myths that are based

on erroneous or outdated information is important. If you don't, the retirement planning that you do for yourself will be founded on assumptions that don't match reality. Projecting ahead into the future and making plans that you have to live with is a risky business under the best—that is, under the most predictable—conditions. But if your predictions are based on faulty assumptions, you can really create problems for yourself and those you love.

Yesterday's thinking hampers planning for tomorrow, and the aging process is already challenging enough—as we'll explore in the next chapter.

2

Preparing for Tomorrow's Reality

Not having enough money during retirement can introduce plenty of anxiety into your life, but one cliche remains true: All the money in the world can't buy happiness. However you define it, happiness is something that resides inside you, which means that you have to give thought to more than just your bank account and investment portfolio in preparing to retire.

So, preparing yourself for retirement isn't only learning about dollars and cents but also about the psychological and physiological changes that you'll experience.

In this chapter we'll discuss some of these psychological and physiological issues. Knowing something about these changes—and why they occur—can help you prepare yourself to deal with them. Perhaps the single most important idea as you read through this chapter is to take a positive view, not a negative one. Know that you can be in control and determine the course of future events.

In the next chapter, we'll talk about developing a spending plan for your retirement. We'll encourage you to look at many categories of current expenses and determine whether they'll go up or down or stay the same in retirement.

This same concept can apply to how you spend your time both today and in retirement. Perhaps your weekday is now filled with preparing for work, working, and, in the evening, some limited community service.

But how will you use your time in retirement? Many people think that being freed from the day-to-day requirements of going to their job will be liberating and provide them the freedom to do the things they always wanted to do. In many cases, this euphoria burns off after the first few months, and then the key question becomes, "What do I do with my time?".

Gone is the network of friends and the opportunity at the water cooler to talk about what each of you are doing. Gone is the sense of personal accomplishment you feel day in and day out doing your job. So, just as you develop a financial plan to meet your desired retirement goals, you must also concurrently plan how you will spend your time. Deciding how you will spend each day is an opportunity to embrace, not a task to be dreaded.

So roll up your sleeves and let's get started.

We'll begin with a brief look—with the help of a number of gerontologists who have served as our advisers—at the aging process.

What body changes may occur?

As we saw in Chapter 1, retirement is usually divided into two stages, the first active, and the second less so. Stage 1 is typically people in their sixties and early seventies and stage 2, people in their late seventies and eighties. In stage 1, you can, with proper diet and exercise, expect to age gradually.

What you're probably most interested in knowing about aging is what's going to happen to you when you reach your seventies and eighties, the second stage of retirement. There are two kinds of changes that take place in the body that are clearly related to aging: functional loss and a reduction in what doctors call homeostasis.

Functional loss involves the gradual reduction of the body's ability to perform certain voluntary and involuntary tasks. For instance, we can lift less weight as we grow older. That's a voluntary action. But the pumping capacity of a human heart—an involuntary action—also declines with age.

The point to remember here is that disease and abuse—smoking, for instance—can also cause loss of function. But even if you never smoke or get sick, just getting older will reduce your ability to do some things.

Homeostasis is, in layperson's terms, the body's ability to maintain normal operating levels. Keeping itself at 98.6 degrees Fahrenheit regardless of its environment is one example of a human body's homeostasis. Maintaining a certain level of sugar in the blood is another. Both of these capabilities, as well as other homeostatic controls, decline with age leaving the elderly, in these two cases, more susceptible to chills or overheating and more prone to develop certain kinds of diabetes.

Other physical changes also relate to aging, but the same changes can come about due to disease or abuse. Separating the effects of aging from these other factors is not always easy.

Cardiovascular changes are clearly age-related. Even a healthy person loses some percentage of his or her heart-lung capabilities with age. Resting heart rate drops and blood pressure rises. The key word here is 'percentage.'' If you've trained your body to run five-mile races at a younger age and you keep up your training, you may still be running these races at age sixty-five. Of course, they'll take a bit more time. But if

you've never been able to run five miles, you won't be able to at sixty-five, either.

Skin changes will take place with age no matter what you do to prevent them. The protective layer of fat just below the skin begins to disappear, and the skin, since it doesn't shrink, wrinkles. Ultraviolet light from a lifetime's exposure to the sun causes skin to lose its elasticity. Diminished activity by sweat and oil glands in the skin cause it to dry out. Nostrums can retard but not prevent what's eventually going to happen. As with running speed, age-related skin changes are all a matter of degree.

Hearing loss gradually occurs with age, although the degree of loss varies greatly. So, too, does the sound frequency at which the loss occurs. Most elderly people suffer the greatest loss at high frequencies where some consonant sounds (z, s, g, f, and t) occur. Others lose their abilities at the opposite end of the sound spectrum. Sometimes older people lose the ability to separate conversation from background noise.

Height and weight can easily change with age. By the time you reach seventy, you may be two inches shorter than you were as a young adult. A lifetime of bad posture is one contributor, but even if you followed your mother's orders to sit up straight and keep your shoulders back, spinal columns compress due to a gradual loss of calcium with age.

As you get shorter you may get fatter—even if you don't eat any more than you used to and even if you keep up the same amount of exercise. That's because the body gradually loses muscle tissue, which is replaced by fat. That in itself doesn't make you heavier, but with the body at rest, fat tissue consumes fewer calories than muscle. So, just conducting the body's normal business requires less food energy (calories) as you get older, and if you don't cut back you will gain weight.

How you can slow the aging process.

So, what can you do during retirement to stay healthier? The first thing you can do is not wait until you retire or wait until you're in your seventies or eighties to ask yourself the question and find some answers.

There is enough literature available on diet and exercise. Get it and read it and apply some common sense. Common sense is important, because a lot of what passes for advice in this area is often subject to fad.

There are dietary changes that you'll have to make as you age to be sure you get the right nutrients. You are going to have to work harder at making sure you get adequate exercise as the pace of your physical activities

slows down. These are things you may have to learn to do. Start learning now.

Taking control

Here's the principal point we'd like you take away from this chapter: There are a great many things you can do to make your life better. You can take control of the quality of your retirement life. Here are a few ideas.

Begin today, while you're still working, to develop outside interests or hobbies. Don't wait until it's too late to discover this truth: If you develop balance among the artistic, family, spiritual, and work dimensions of your life, you'll feel better about yourself as you grow older. Too many people think work is all there is. They learn the sad truth—that a full and satisfying life requires all these facets—after they retire.

Begin to do volunteer work. Most retired people who feel successful have become involved in doing something for others.

Plan to learn something new. Many retirees are finding out that it's never too late to learn. And it's fun as well. Moreover, formal programs have been developed to accommodate this thirst for learning. One very successful program is Elderhostel, a Boston-based group, that last year signed up close to 200,000 students age sixty and up in classes ranging from "Prehistoric Art of Southwest New Mexico" to "How to Ring English Handbells.' Colleges and cultural institutions around the world host these week-long classes for older people, even when regular classes are still in session. The average cost comes to a modest $240, including room and board.

Plan for the fact that more women than men will live to enjoy retirement. One-third of baby boomers will likely live to age eighty-five. However, there is no demographic evidence to suggest that the difference in longevity between men and women will evaporate. According to American Demographics magazine, women will account for 60 percent of aged boomers.

Don't count on your children taking care of you. In the first place, as many as 20 percent of baby-boomers don't have children. Also, it's a poor idea to count on your children supporting you in your old age. The truth is that future retirees will have to shell out for many services that family members have traditionally provided for nothing.

And that final point brings us back to the subject at hand: financial planning for retirement.

3

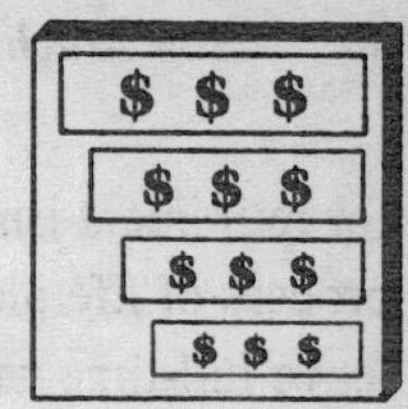

How Much Will You Need for Retirement?

To paraphrase English philosopher Bertrand Russell, what most of us hope to have in retirement is enough money to meet our wants and needs, whatever they are, and enough leisure time to enjoy it.

This is not an unreasonable goal for a great many people and especially not—we're going to say this so often you'll probably become heartily sick of hearing it—for people who start their retirement planning process soon enough. In fact, the first part of that process consists of asking yourself what it is that you will want during retirement and then calculating the amount of money you're going to need at retirement to get it.

As we tried to make clear in the last chapter, planning

for retirement isn't so much a financial exercise as it is a process of life planning. How you want to live once you leave full-time work will determine much about how you go about getting ready for retirement.

A word about inflation is demanded in any discussion of retirement financial planning. You ignore inflation, which can be a pesky little varmint or a ravenous beast, at your peril. In the United States, most economists feel that inflation will remain low over the next 20 or so years, averaging somewhere in the 4-to-6 percent range. But don't be lulled into thinking that this low rate doesn't affect you.

Let's say that you expect to draw a $30,000 pension over a 20-year retirement period, and let's say that inflation averages just 4 percent. In twenty years, the buying power of your $30,000 pension will have been cut to $13,700. If your pension is not indexed to rise with inflation, you're going to need other money put aside and invested in order to maintain the $30,000 buying power you started out with. And not just a little extra money, either. In our example, you'll have to accumulate an additional $111,000 and invest it at 8 percent just to offset the effects of inflation over that 20-year period.

Some of the income you expect to live on after retirement may already be tied to the inflation rate in one way or another. Social Security payments to retirees are adjusted for inflation by law. And if you continue to work, even part time, after retiring, your compensation from the job will also be adjusted upward with inflation. A job that pays $15 an hour when you first take it might pay $20 an hour five years later.

If you're relying on a defined-contribution plan, which gives you a lump-sum settlement upon retirement, then, naturally, the income available to you will reflect the investment choices you make after retirement. Your investments, presumably, will respond in some way to the then current inflation rate.

The point we'd like you to remember about inflation is just this: Any pension, investment, or salary that doesn't rise each year by at least the rate of inflation is actually reducing the purchasing power of your retirement income.

How much is enough?

Remember that back in Chapter 1 we suggested that you think about retirement as having two phases: an active phase followed by an inactive one. When you begin making calculations, as we will momentarily, about the amount of money you'll need to achieve the lifestyle you want in retirement, make those calculations based on your plans for the active period of your retirement. You don't know, and it's impossible to predict, what your expenses will be during the second, inactive period, but odds are they'll be less. You want to base your planning on the more expensive of the two.

First, we're going to help you figure out what you want to spend during your retirement years. Then we'll show you how to calculate the amount you need to put aside to support that planned spending.

The best way of estimating what you're going to spend after retirement is to start with what you're spending now. Presumably, you'll at least want to maintain the same standard of living. Anyway, you should start there and make adjustments. For the moment, don't worry about inflation. Just use current dollars in your estimates. In a later chapter we'll show you how to build in an adjustment for inflation.

In Appendix I, you'll find a retirement cash-flow worksheet. As you read to the end of this chapter, you should then turn to the appendix and use it to help you make your retirement expense analysis. We also provide an example to help you complete your own worksheet.

How much should you adjust your current spending figures to reflect your post-retirement needs? It varies with the item. If you expect to remain in the same house that you're now in and if the mortgage will be paid off by then, you can eliminate that expense. Job-related expenses, such as clothing and entertaining, will go down. But leisure-time expenses, such as travel and golf fees, may go up. Will your children be grown and educated? Then the cost of feeding and clothing them will probably have disappeared. You may need less life insurance then, but you may have to purchase more expensive health insurance.

For each expense item on the worksheet make the best estimate you can about how it will change after you've quit working. After you're done you'll know what you think you want to spend annually during retirement. The question now becomes: How much do I need to put aside to assure that I can cover those expenses?

That's what we'll help you figure out in the next chapter.

4

Getting What You Need

Okay, you have forecasted the expense side of your retirement budget. That is, by now you have a pretty good idea of what you're going to want to spend once you quit working full time.

The next step is to calculate where you stand financially today. Turn to Appendix VIII. There you'll find a net worth worksheet to fill out.

Now the question is, how do you get from where you are financially to where you want to be? Or, put another way, how do you get what you need?

Too many people at this point jump ahead of themselves. They think that the task facing them is to identify, then implement specific savings and investment plans.

Eventually that's true, but there's an intervening step. It's important, before you start calling your investment broker or accountant, to understand what your specific goals are—and why. That's because later, once you've put one or another strategy into action, you need to check periodically to see not only whether it's working, but whether the objectives of that strategy still meet your needs.

In other words, you need to understand that good retirement financial planning is not something that you do once. Rather, it's a process that continues until that day when there's no more retirement to plan for. And the process comes down to asking yourself three basic questions—What do I have? What do I want? How do I get what I want?—in ever-increasing detail.

You can go through this exercise at any time, and you should go through it often, not only when one of the elements of your retirement plan changes—when, for instance, you change jobs—but periodically, even if you're not aware of a change, just to check your assumptions.

To see how the process works and how you can use it to make sure that your own plan, once it's formulated

and in place, is still valid, take the time to go through this illustrative example with us.

We've developed an easy to use worksheet to help you estimate how much you need to set aside each year to meet your retirement goal. What follows is a sample worksheet with answers provided for a hypothetical couple, Stan and Rhonda. Read through the pages that follow, and you'll see how to fill out your own worksheet, which we've provided in Appendix II.

Before we begin, though, a few facts about Stan and Rhonda: Stan and Rhonda are both 45 years old and want to retire in 20 years at age 65 with a comfortable lifestyle. They're planning on a long retirement—25 years or until the age of 90—and they're conservative investors.

In both the sample worksheet and the worksheet we've provided for you to fill out, we've used two broad assumptions: One is that long-term inflation will average 4 percent annually. We believe that this rate is a realistic one for the next 15 to 30 years. Two is that you'll use both the earnings on your investments and the principal to fund your retirement years. We use this assumption, known as annuitization, because it results in having to save less for retirement although the tradeoff is that there is less to pass on to your heirs.

Worksheet To Estimate Retirement Needs

Annual Retirement Income Goal (in Today's Dollars) (See Appendix I)	(A)	$ 63,000
Estimated Social Security Benefits (See Appendix III)	(B)	(21,000)
Pension Income	(C)	(30,000)
Income Needed from Assets in Today's Dollars (A) − (B) − (C)	(D)	$ 12,000
Income Needed from Assets At Retirement (adjusted for Inflation) (D) × Factor 1 (Appendix IV)	(E)	$ 26,300
Capital Needed to Fund Income for Retirement Period (E) × Factor 2 (Appendix V)	(F)	$433,700
Additional Capital Needed to Maintain Purchasing Power of Pension if not Adjusted for Inflation:		
Value of Pension at Retirement (C) × Factor 1 (Appendix IV)	(G)	$ 65,700
Capital Needed to Maintain Purchasing Power of Pension (G) × Factor 3 (Appendix V)	(H)	325,900

Total Capital Required at Beginning of Retirement (F) + (H)	(I)	$759,600
Current Assets that are Available to fund Retirement (current value of 401(k)s, IRAs, Profit Sharing Plans, and personal investments) (see Net Worth Statement in Appendix VIII)	(J)	$117,000
Value of those assets at Retirement (J) × Factor 4 (Appendix VI)	(K)	545,200
Additional Capital Required at Retirement (I) − (K)	(L)	$214,400

If this number is negative, stop here—you do not have to save additional amounts for retirement.

Amount to be saved each year to meet retirement goal (L) × Factor 5 (Appendix VII)	(M)	$ 4,700

- HOW MUCH INCOME DO I NEED TO MAINTAIN THIS "COMFORTABLE LIFESTYLE"?

Line A: Use the figure you previously calculated in Appendix I—in Stan and Rhonda's case, about $63,000 annually.

- HOW MUCH OF THAT INCOME IS REASONABLY ASSURED ALREADY?

In other words, how much do I have now?

Line B: Social Security should pay Stan and Rhonda about $21,000 a year. To estimate your Social Security benefits, turn to Appendix III. (We've provided estimated annual benefits at normal retirement age and at age 62. The estimates for the spousal benefit assume a non-working spouse who is the same age as you.)

Line C: From Stan's company-sponsored pension plan, he can project income of $30,000 a year. So, the total income they can expect now at age sixty-five comes to $51,000—$30,000 plus $21,000.

Line D: That leaves Stan and Rhonda short $12,000.

- WHAT DO I NEED?

Line E: Stan and Rhonda need to generate an additional $12,000 a year in income. They understand that these numbers are in current dollars so they need to convert them to future dollars. We've provided a table in Appendix IV for just this purpose. The table assumes a 4% rate of inflation. You find the number of years until you retire in the first column. Then, multiply the factor printed in the second column times Line D. In Stan and

Rhonda's case they multiply 2.19 times $12,000 to get $26,300.

• HOW DO I GET WHAT I NEED?

Line F: To generate $26,300 in annual income requires capital of $433,700 invested at a conservative 8 percent. How did Stan and Rhonda arrive at that figure? They used Factor 2 listed in Appendix V. First you look up how long you'll be in retirement—25 years in the case of Stan and Rhonda. Next, you decide what rate of return you'll earn on your investments while you're retired. Third, where these two lines meet is the factor you'll use for this calculation.

Line G and Line H: Stan and Rhonda also need to protect the buying power of Stan's pension, which, in this example, unlike Social Security isn't indexed for inflation. That is, they need additional dollars to compensate for the effects of inflation on Stan's pension. To protect his $30,000 pension, which in 20 years will be worth $65,700, they need to accumulate an additional $325,900. To inflate the pension, you apply the same factor 1 you used for Line E. To determine the amount you need for Line H, use factor 3 in Appendix V. You perform this calculation the same way you did the calculation for Line F.

So Stan and Rhonda need a total of $759,600—that is, Line F plus Line H—by the time they retire.

• WHAT DO I HAVE NOW?

Line J: Stan and Rhonda use their net worth worksheet in Appendix VIII to determine what assets they'll use for retirement. Stan's 401(k) balance stands at $55,000 and his IRA at $12,000. Stan and Rhonda's personal assets add up to $50,000 for a total of $117,000.

Line K: So then if they assume these amounts will increase at a rate of 8 percent annually, these dollars will be worth $545,200 by the time they retire. They calculated this amount by multiplying factor 4 from Appendix VI times $117,000, Line J.

Line L: Stan and Rhonda need to accumulate $214,400—that is, $759,600, Line I minus $545,200, Line K—in additional savings by the time they retire.

Line M: If they assume that their savings will earn 8 percent annually between now and retirement, they must put away $4,700 per year for the next 20 years in order to meet their income goal. They use factor 5 in Appendix VII to figure this amount.

See how the process—simple as it is—works? Not

until you've gone through this process of figuring out what your specific goals are—or of checking up on them from time to time—are you ready to start planning and implementing a savings and investment strategy.

The key is to ask the broad questions first, then keep narrowing down. The advantage to this approach is that you end up with manageable problems to solve.

In the example above, we went from asking how we were ever going to generate enough income to retire to the specific need of putting aside enough savings to produce just $12,000 in additional retirement income. If you don't break the task down, it seems Herculean and therefore too discouraging even to contemplate.

Furthermore, breaking the retirement planning task down into small, specific elements makes the plan easier to reevaluate from time to time. You need only to check on the continuing validity of each simple element. If they're all working, then your whole plan remains valid. If one element has changed, you know by what amount you need to compensate.

In summary, several of these key elements are:

- When do you want to retire?
- How much do you want to live on?

- How long do you think your retirement will last?
- How much do you currently have set aside?
- What investment rate do you want to use?

In the next chapters, we'll look at specific investments and strategies to help you reach the financial cushion you need for a secure retirement.

5

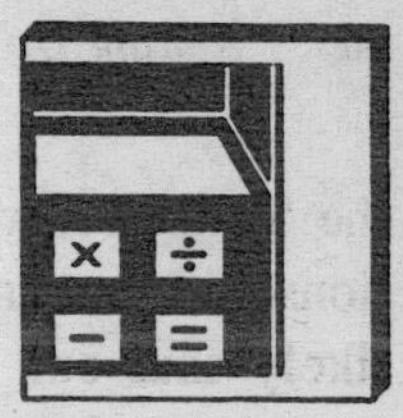

Adding Up Your Social Security Benefits

When our lawmakers adopted the 1935 Social Security Act, their intention was to provide retirement benefits for working Americans. Since that time, a lot has changed. Today, Social Security provides retirement benefits not only for wage earners but for their spouses and dependents as well. In addition, Social Security programs, such as Medicare, cover many medical costs of Americans sixty-five years of age or older.

How much in Social Security benefits can you expect to pocket when you retire? That's what this chapter is all about. First, though, a quick word to the wise. From time to time, federal budget watchers forecast an end to the Social Security system. Don't let their dire predictions of doom and gloom worry you. It's extremely unlikely that our legislators would ever permit Social Security to fail.

Maybe, though, you're not that pessimistic. Like many people, you think the system will stay intact, but you fear you'll never get back from Social Security the amounts you paid in. Well, that's not true either, and here are the numbers to prove it.

Say you started working at age twenty-five, you're married, your spouse doesn't work outside the home, and you retire at age sixty-five. Say, too, that you paid the maximum Social Security tax every year. Here's how your benefits would add up:

	Current Age			
	65	*62*	*55*	*45*
Total Social Security tax paid through age 65	$41,300	$52,900	$79,800	$116,800
Projected joint benefit	$17,700	$17,400	$19,300	$21,000

Now, how long will it take you to recoup the total amount of Social Security taxes you've paid over the years?

The answer is not long, as the following chart illustrates.

	Current Age 65	62	55	45
Number of years it takes to recoup your total Social Security taxes	2.33	3.04	4.13	5.56

But wait a minute you say. What if I'd invested the amount I paid in Social Security taxes instead of sending the money to Uncle Sam? In the long run, you'll still pocket more with Social Security, as we show in the following chart.

	Current Age 65	62	55	45
Number of years it takes to recoup the total amount of Social Security taxes you paid through age 65 if you'd invested these dollars at a real rate of return of 4 percent	3.46	4.65	7.00	11.22

What's the bottom line? Social Security is a better deal than most of us imagine.

Why are your earnings important?

It's simple. The more you make, the more you'll pocket in Social Security benefits. The law bases your benefits on your average earnings for the highest 35 of 40 years during your lifetime.

Who keeps track of your earnings?

The Office of Central Operations of the Social Security Administration keeps an earnings report on every American who has a Social Security number. Employers—and in the case of self-employed people the IRS—send reports of earnings to this central office.

How can you check your earnings record?

All you need to do is fill out and mail Form SSA-7004-PC, "'Request for Earnings and Benefit Estimate Statement," and mail it to the Social Security Administration. The address is Social Security Administration, Wilkes-Barre Data Operations Center, P.O. Box 20, Wilkes-Barre, PA 18711.

You can obtain a copy of this form from your local Social Security Administration office or U.S. post office. Or simply make a copy of the form that we provide in the appendix.

Once the Social Security Administration receives your form, it will send you a statement of the wages and self-employment income credited to you.

Why check your earnings record?

It's a good idea to check your earnings records, because errors have been known to happen. So check your earnings statement carefully, especially if you've changed employers or if you have more than one company.

What if you weren't credited for some of your earnings?

If you find that some of your earnings weren't credited to you, don't wait. Contact your local Social Security office at once to get the problem corrected.

Do you need to check your earnings record often?

You do—even if you're many years away from retirement. The fact is, you should confirm your earnings history with the Social Security Administration every three years or so.

Social Security may have trouble rectifying errors that occurred many years ago. If you identify a mistake early on, you'll be able to fix it.

Are you eligible for Social Security benefits?

Uncle Sam says you're eligible for benefits if you are—in the jargon of the Social Security Administration—"fully insured." As far as the government is concerned, you're fully insured as long as you've built up a certain number of "calendar quarters of coverage."

What's a calendar quarter?

A calendar quarter is credited for every $520 you earn during a year up to a maximum of four quarters each year.

Are you fully insured?

To be fully insured—that is, entitled to full Social Security benefits—you must have 40 quarters of coverage (a total of 10 years' work). Once you've acquired the 40 quarters, you're fully insured for life—and entitled to benefits even if you never work again. If you're born before 1929 you need fewer than 40 quarters to qualify. Check with your local Social Security office to determine the exact number.

How are your Social Security benefits calculated?

Since 1979, the Social Security Administration has used a method known as wage indexing to compute the benefits it pays. This method bases the retirement benefit you'd receive on your "indexed" earnings over a fixed period of years after 1950.

Only earnings credited to your Social Security account are used. In the table below are the maximum earnings Social Security will credit for specific years.

Year	Earnings
1990	$51,300
1989	$48,000
1988	45,000
1987	43,800
1986	42,000
1985	39,600
1984	37,800
1983	35,700
1982	32,400
1981	29,700
1980	25,900
1979	22,900
1978	17,700
1977	16,500
1976	15,300
1975	14,100
1974	13,200

(continued)

Year	Earnings
1973	10,800
1972	9,000
1968 to 1971	7,800
1966 to 1967	6,600
1959 to 1965	4,800
1955 to 1958	4,200
1951 to 1954	3,600

But what if you just need a rough estimate of your retirement benefits? Even if you're years away from retiring, the Social Security Administration will—upon request—provide you with an estimate of your monthly benefits.

Again, just fill out and mail Form SSA-7004-PC, "Request for Social Security Earnings and Benefit Estimate Statement." (You'll find a copy of this form in the appendix.) When they receive your form, Social Security Administration officials will send you an estimate of your benefits in addition to providing you with your earnings record.

If you want a faster answer, just look at Appendix III. You'll find a table that lists average annual earnings and the estimated benefits you can expect to receive.

As you'll see, if you retired in 1990 at the age of sixty-five, the most you can expect to receive would be about $11,800—$5,900 for your spouse, if he or she doesn't work outside the home and is also age 65—or a total of $17,700 if you're married. You'd receive less if you retired and collected Social Security benefits in 1990 at the age of sixty-two—about $9,000 for you, $4,200 for your spouse, or a total of $13,200. That's because Uncle Sam allows you, at age sixty-two, to collect only 80 percent of the benefits to which you'd be entitled if you'd retired at age sixty-five.

Where can you write for additional information?

If you'd like to know more about Social Security, ask the Social Security Administration for copies of its Publication 05-10035, Your Social Security, and its Publication 05-10077, Your Social Security Rights and Responsibilities. Both are free of charge. You may telephone the Social Security Administration—the toll-free number is (800) 234-5772—or, if you prefer, you may write the Social Security Administration, Department of Health and Human Services, Baltimore, MD 21235.

If you'd like to receive news updates from Social Security—they're known officially as Social Security Information Items—write the Social Security Administration, Office of Information, Room 4-J-10

West High Rise, 6401 Security Blvd., Baltimore, MD 21235.

Social Security benefits, of course, provide only one part of your retirement income. In the next chapter, we'll take a look at company retirement plans.

6

Cashing in on Company Retirement and Savings Plans

If you're like most people, your company retirement and savings plan will be an important source of income for you one day. What do you need to know when it comes to your employer-sponsored retirement plan? That's what this chapter is all about.

Let's start, though, with a few basics.

When you look at company retirement plans, you need to focus on these three questions: who contributes to the plan, what happens to the money in the plan, and how do you take your money out. We'll cover the last topic—how do you take your money out—in Chapters 21 and 22. In this chapter, we'll focus on the first two issues.

How do defined-benefit plans work?

With a defined-benefit plan, your employer typically makes all the contributions. You collect a set amount each month from the day you retire—regardless of how much money was put away for you or how the investments in the plan performed.

The set amount you receive each month is determined by a formula, which is outlined in the summary plan description of your pension plan. This summary is distributed to all employees. The following chart is a highly simplified example of how the formula works.

As the chart shows, three main items determine how much you will receive from a defined-benefit plan: your salary, your length of service with the company, and the "factor" or percentage that your plan's formula uses.

Depending on the plan, your final average salary may be determined by your highest five years, the highest five out of the last 10 years, your career average, and so forth.

The factor is simply a number—in our example, 1.5%—or numbers that are applied to the final average salary. In most cases, a plan uses two or three different factors, most of them based on Social Security earnings. In our example, though, we've generalized to one average factor.

Final average salary (FAS)	$80,000
Total years of credited service	30

Calculation:

*1.5% × years of service × average total compensation (1.5% × 30 × $80,000)	$36,000
Estimated single life benefit	$36,000
Estimated joint-and survivor 50% benefit	$32,400

* Average factor per year of service

You should know that "single life" is an annuity payment that is calculated on the basis of the employee's life expectancy. A "joint-and-survivor" annuity, by contrast, is based on the life expectancy of the employee and his or her spouse or other beneficiary. With a joint-and-survivor annuity, the surviving spouse continues to receive payments until he or she dies. So the amount paid initially is less because the time period for payment is potentially longer.

The chart shows how the formula works for a person who's retiring at the normal retirement age of 65. But what would happen if he or she retired at age sixty instead?

Many companies "discount" your pension by a certain percentage per month if you retire early. So say, in our example, that the company discounts your pension by 0.25 percent per month for each month that you retire before normal retirement age of 65. So if you retire at age 60, you would lose 15 percent of your pension—that is, 12 months times five years times 0.25 percent per month.

Where will the money come from to pay your benefits? Each year a company is told by its actuaries what future pension benefits are payable and the extent to which current plan assets and future investment earnings meet these obligations. If this analysis shows a shortfall, the company must make additional current contributions. What if the plan's assets exceed future obligations? The company does not need to make current contributions. Thus, the more the plan earns on its investments, the less the company may have to contribute.

With a defined-benefit plan, your employer isn't obligated to provide you with a projection of your benefits at retirement, but many companies do.

The problem with these estimates? The company often bases them on its own assumptions, not yours. Your employer, for example, might provide you with an estimate of your retirement benefits only for age 65. You, however, plan to retire at age 62. Or the company might give you an estimate based on your life expectancy only, not the life expectancy of you and your spouse.

However, your company's human resources department might be able to help you obtain an estimate of your benefits tailored to your own needs.

How do defined-contribution plans work?

With a defined-contribution plan, you or your company,—or you *and* your company—sock away a set amount annually—2 percent of your wages, say. And the amount you pocket when you retire depends not only on the amount that was put away but how well those dollars were invested.

Defined-contribution plans themselves come in a number of varieties. And many companies allow employees to participate in more than one type of plan.

The most common defined-contribution plans are profit-sharing plans, employee thrift plans, money purchase plans, stock bonus plans, and employee stock ownership plans.

What is a profit-sharing plan?

By definition, a profit-sharing plan is an agreement between a company and its employees that allows workers to share in company profits. It used to be that your company could make contributions to such a plan only if it posted a profit—but no more.

Nowadays, a company may make contributions to a profit-sharing plan even if it reports no earnings. Also, as in the past, it may change the percentage of its contributions from one year to the next.

An employer may also calculate its contributions using a formula that takes a number of factors into account, including the amount you earn each year. The rules say, however, that the employer's contribution generally may not top 15 percent of the compensation of all workers.

Here's an example.

Say your employer will contribute 10 percent of its profits to its employees' retirement accounts. The company's earnings that year equal $1 million, so it plans to contribute a total of $100,000.

However, the total compensation of its workforce comes to only $500,000. That means the company's total contribution for the year is limited to $75,000 (15 percent times $500,000), and your share is reduced proportionally. The $25,000 difference gets carried over to the following year.

With a profit-sharing plan, the company—not you—often decides how the money in the plan is invested.

What are 401(k) plans?

Employee thrift and savings plans—or 401(k)s, as they're usually known—are also defined-contribution plans. Here's how they work. You contribute a portion of your after-tax earnings to the plan, and your employer may match all or a portion of your contributions. You decide how the contributions are invested, choosing from among the vehicles your employer makes available to you. We detail 401(k) plans in the next chapter.

What are money purchase plans?

Money purchase plans—unlike employee thrift and savings plans—are considered pension plans. That's because the company has a fixed obligation under the plan to make contributions—whether or not it posts a profit.

The amount an employer contributes to a money purchase plan is based on a percentage of the compensation of all participants. But the most, by law, a company may contribute is 25 percent of the earnings of employees who participate in all the employer's defined-contribution plans.

Again, the company—not you—often decides how the money in the plan is invested.

What are employee stock ownership plans?

These plans, familiarly known as ESOPs, invest in the stock of the company that sponsors the plan. So the growth of the stock in the plan—and therefore, your retirement benefit—depends on how well your company performs.

You should know, though, that the ESOP rules say that when you reach the age of fifty-five, you may diversify a portion of your account into other investments. (A similar rule applies to other retirement plans, such as profit-sharing plans, that invest primarily in company stock.)

Does Uncle Sam cap contributions to these plans?

The answer is yes. The ceiling is the lesser of 25 percent of your annual earnings or $30,000 (which is 25

percent of $120,000). And this cap applies to *all* your defined-contribution plans.

In other words, if you participate in two plans—a profit-sharing plan and an employee stock ownership plan, say—no more than a *total* of $30,000 or 25 percent of your annual earnings, whichever is less, could be put away in your behalf.

How do you get an estimate of your benefits from a defined-contribution plan?

If you participate in a defined-contribution plan, your company must notify you of your account balance at least once a year.

In the next chapter, we'll look at one of the best of the defined-contribution plans—the 401(k).

7

Get Smart About 401(k)s

Never heard of a 401(k) plan?

Then you may want to listen up.

As you may remember, retirement plans to which the employee, not the employer, takes the lead in contributing are becoming increasingly prominent today. The 401(k) is among the best of these so-called defined contribution plans.

Why 401(k)? The term 401(k) just refers to the section of the Internal Revenue Code that created these tax-favored, company-sponsored retirement savings programs. As we'll explain in this chapter, they're actually quite terrific.

Why participate in a 401(k)?

There are lots of reasons to take part in your company-sponsored 401(k) plan. One is to slash your current tax bill. Another is the opportunity to build retirement savings on a tax deferred basis. Still another is to boost the amount of money you collect from your employer.

A 401(k)—like an IRA—is a tax-deferred savings vehicle. You pay no income taxes on the dollars you contribute until they're withdrawn, usually at retirement.

And your interest, dividends, and other earnings accumulate tax deferred until you take them out—again, usually at retirement.

So you build up your retirement nest egg—and accumulate wealth—faster than you would with a savings account that wasn't tax-favored.

How much faster? Let's take a look.

Suppose it's 1990, and you're a taxpayer in the 28 percent marginal bracket. Each year for 25 years, you plan to sock away $7,000 of your earnings in an investment yielding an average annual return of 8 percent. Actually, though, you have only $5,040 to put away.

Why $5,040? You pay income taxes on your earnings, and those taxes add up to a $1,960 a year—that is, 28 percent times $7,000.

At the end of 25 years—after you pay your taxes each

year—your investment will have grown to a hefty $282,750. Not bad, you say, and you're right, but wait.

What if you set aside the same amount in your employer-sponsored 401(k)? And what if your dollars earned the same return—8 percent annually for 25 years?

With your money in a 401(k), the earnings build up tax deferred. Also, you have the full $7,000 to put away. In 25 years, you'd have salted away an impressive $552,680—$269,930 more—and that's not small change.

But you should remember that *tax deferred* isn't the same as *tax free*. The dollars you put away in a 401(k) are taxable when they're withdrawn, so you don't escape taxes entirely with these plans. You simply postpone them for a while.

However, even after paying taxes at 28 percent, you'd have $397,930, or $115,180 more than the investment you'd have outside the 401(k). Moreover, this example doesn't even take into account any money your employer may contribute to your 401(k). As we'll see, a 401(k) is an even better deal if your company matches a portion of your contribution.

How can you use a 401(k) to capture additional dollars from your company? The fact is many employers—

maybe yours is one of them—match the amount employees put away in these plans. For example, your employer may contribute 50 cents for every dollar you set aside. Usually, however, employers cap their contributions to the first 3 percent to 6 percent of the amount you contribute.

For most people, a key reason for participating in an employer-sponsored 401(k) savings plan is to collect the additional amounts from your company. After all, if your employer kicks in 50 cents for every dollar you contribute, you're immediately getting a 50 percent return on your investment.

How does a 401(k) work?

First, you instruct your company to subtract an agreed-upon sum from your check every pay period and deposit that amount in a 401(k) account that bears your name.

Uncle Sam omits these deferred earnings—and any interest, dividends, and capital gains that accumulate in the account—from current taxation. Don't worry, the federal government gets what it's owed—but not until you take your dollars out of your 401(k), in most cases, at retirement.

Does this scenario seem familiar? It should, because

401(k)s are a lot like IRAs. The difference between the two plans lies in the way Uncle Sam treats the money you deposit.

Under the rules, you don't deduct your 401(k) contribution on your Form 1040. Instead, the dollars you sock away in a 401(k) are treated as *deferred compensation*; that is, the money isn't listed as income to you on your W-2 Form.

Suppose your pay adds up to $40,000 in 1990, and you deposit 5 percent of that amount, or $2,000, in your company's 401(k). When you get your W-2 form, it lists your income as $38,000—your earnings of $40,000 *less* your $2,000 contribution to the 401(k).

You should know that the dollars you contribute to a 401(k) aren't exempt from Social Security (FICA) payroll taxes. That news isn't all bad, though.

Why? When it comes time to calculate your Social Security benefits, the government takes into account the amount of Social Security taxes you've paid.

The more you've paid, the more you receive.

How much may you contribute?

Uncle Sam sets two ceilings on 401(k) contributions. The first applies to you, the employee; the second to your employer. Under the first, you may put aside no more than $7,979 in pretax contributions in a 401(k) plan in 1990. (This amount is adjusted annually for inflation.)

The second rule—the one governing employers—is more complicated. It says that the two of you—meaning you and your company—may not jointly sock away more than $30,000, or 25 percent of your compensation, whichever is less.

Where may you invest the dollars you contribute to your 401(k)?

You've wisely decided to stash cash in a 401(k). So, you ask, now what? You must learn how to manage the account, since all the investment decisions are yours to make.

The law doesn't impose many limitations on the kinds of investments you may make with the money deposited in your employer-sponsored 401(k) plan.

You're restricted only by the investments your company makes available to you. In other words, you may invest only in the vehicles the company offers.

In most cases, these investments include equity mutual funds, shares of stock in your company, money-market accounts, annuities and other insurance products, and government securities, such as Treasury bills.

In fact, most 401(k)s allow you to choose among at least three investment vehicles, although the law doesn't require employers to offer that many. Some companies permit you to put your dollars into any or all of the investments available, while others limit your options.

Will your 401(k) contribution affect your benefits?

It may, and here's why.

Say your company provides you with a whole host of fringes—disability insurance, survivor income, and so on—and these benefits are based on your salary.

Say, too, that your company provides you with a life insurance policy that has a face value equal to twice your annual salary—$100,000 in your case.

Under the rules, your company may calculate the value of that insurance policy by multiplying two times your annual compensation *before* your 401(k) contribution ($100,000) or two times your annual compensation after your 401(k) contribution ($92,000).

Likewise, your company may figure your pension benefits based on your salary before or after your annual 401(k) contribution.

Uncle Sam does allow your employer to change its definition of *compensation* in its retirement and other benefit plans in order to count dollars you set aside in your 401(k). That means you won't forfeit some of your benefits by contributing to a 401(k).

But the choice is your company's to make.

What if you work for a public institution?

The law doesn't allow people employed by colleges, universities, and other public institutions to participate in 401(k)s. But this rule doesn't mean you're out in the cold when it comes to saving for retirement. You can participate in what's known as a 403(b) plan.

How do these tax-deferred savings plans work? As with 401(k)s, an agreed-upon sum is subtracted from your check every pay period and deposited in a 403(b) account. You're not currently taxed on that amount. Also as with a 401(k), the dollars you set aside, plus any earnings that accumulate, build up tax deferred until they're withdrawn, usually at retirement.

Uncle Sam caps your annual deductible contributions to a 403(b) at $9,500 or 20 percent of your earnings each year, whichever is less.

If your company offers a 401(k) should you participate?

Make no mistake about it. A 401(k) is one of the best places you have available to you to save for retirement. As we saw, in addition to tax-deferred saving, you often get a matching contribution from your employer and excellent investment options. A 401(k) is also convenient and easy, because your employer withdraws the money directly from your paycheck.

So if your employer offers a 401(k), go for it. You have virtually nothing to lose and almost everything to gain.

We've mentioned IRAs in this chapter. In the next chapter, we'll take a detailed look at these retirement savings accounts.

8

Why IRAs Are Still a Great Way to Save

Sure, Individual Retirement Accounts (IRAs) have lost some of their luster, but they can still be a stepping stone to a comfortable retirement. How? In this chapter, we'll take a look at these retirement savings vehicles to see what they'll do for you.

Is your IRA contribution deductible?

Figuring out whether you may deduct your IRA contribution isn't hard. In fact, it's simple. Here are the rules.

If neither you nor your spouse is an active participant in a company pension or profit-sharing plan, you may stash away and deduct up to $2,000 for yourself and an additional $250 for a spouse who doesn't work outside the home. And this rule holds true regardless of your income.

Now, what if you or your spouse actively participates in an employer-sponsored pension plan? Then another set of regulations apply.

Uncle Sam says that if you're single, you may pocket a full deduction only if your adjusted gross income (AGI) is $25,000 or less. Your allowable deduction drops $10 for each $50 you earn above $25,000 until you hit $35,000, when the deduction phases out entirely.

If you're married and file jointly and either one of you is an active participant in a company plan, you're entitled to a full deduction only if your AGI is $40,000 or less. Your deduction also declines $10 for each additional $50 in income up to $50,000, when the deduction vanishes. Filing separately won't help. If married couples who live together file separately, no deduction is allowable to either person.

How do you know if you're an active participant?

Take a peek at your W-2 form. It includes a box entitled "pension plan" for your employer to check. If the

IRA

box is checked, you know you're an active participant. What if this box is blank? Roll up your sleeves, because you have some work to do. You'll need a thorough grounding in what's known as the active participation rules.

Uncle Sam says it makes no difference whether you actually participate in a defined-benefit retirement plan. It matters only that you're *eligible* to participate.

However, the rules are different for a defined-contribution plan. With a defined-contribution plan, you're considered an active participant if—during the year—you or your company contribute money to the plan on your behalf.

But Uncle Sam does carve out one important exception to this rule. He says that you're not an active participant if the only money that gets added on your behalf during the year are earnings from the investments already in the plan.

What if you're not vested?

When it comes to the active participation rules, it makes no difference whether you're vested—that is, eligible to receive future benefits from a plan.

Say, for example, that your company contributes an

amount each year in your name to its defined-contribution plan. Say, also, that the plan rules state that you aren't vested until you've worked for the company for a full three years. As far as the IRS is concerned, you're an active participant even if you aren't vested.

What if you participate for only part of the year?

In the eyes of the IRS, you're an active participant if you take part in a retirement plan for just part of the year.

What counts as a qualified retirement plan?

When it comes to the active-participation rules, several types of plans fall into the category of qualified or tax-favored plans.

If you participate in any one of them, the law considers you an active participant, and that means you can't deduct your IRA contribution—unless your AGI falls below certain levels.

What counts as a qualified plan? Any of these plans are considered qualified: qualified pension, profit-sharing, or stock bonus plans, including Keogh plans; 401(k)

IRA

plans and simplified employee pension plans (SEPs); and retirement plans for federal, state, or local government employees.

Still other plans that fall into this category are: tax-sheltered annuities for public school teachers, employees of charitable organizations, deferred compensation plans for state employees and certain union plans.

How many IRAs may you have?

Uncle Sam doesn't care if you set up one IRA or a dozen or a hundred. And you may set them up at as many different financial institutions as you want, as long as you qualify.

However, be careful when you open multiple accounts. Most institutions charge you annual fees, which can run up to $50 or more, to maintain your IRA. So if you maintain many small accounts—and they all charge fees—your effective yield drops. Uncle Sam does let you deduct the annual maintenance fee. But you may write it off only if you pay it out of separate funds, not the IRA funds, and it and all other miscellaneous itemized deductions top 2 percent of your adjusted gross income.

Who serves as the trustee of your IRA?

The manager of your IRA may be the institution or institutions where you maintain IRA accounts: a bank, savings and loan, insurance company, and so forth. You may also manage your account yourself, investing as you see fit. If that's your preference, you'd use a brokerage house, say, as custodian of your IRA.

Where may you invest your IRA dollars?

Your strategy for investing your IRA funds should be the same as your strategy for investing all your other retirement dollars.

You can invest your IRA in most regular investment vehicles—certificates of deposit, mutual funds, stocks, or zero-coupon bonds, for example.

However, you don't have total freedom when it comes to investing your IRA dollars. Buying a life insurance contract is out. Art objects, antiques, gold or silver coins (except gold and silver coins minted in the U.S.), stamps, or other collectibles are also forbidden when it comes to IRAs.

If you should use IRA dollars to invest in collectibles, Uncle Sam treats the amount you invested as a withdrawal from your account. That means you must pay tax on that amount at ordinary rates. There's more bad news. If you invested in the collectible before age fifty-nine and one-half, you must fork over an additional 10 percent penalty.

There's one more investment you should avoid when it comes to your IRA dollars—municipal bonds. Here's the reason: As you know, Uncle Sam taxes the money in your IRA account when you withdraw it. Municipal bonds are tax-free. So by putting these bonds in your IRA account, you're converting tax-free income into taxable income.

May you switch from one investment to another?

You say you want to switch your IRA dollars from one investment vehicle—bonds, say—to another, stocks, for example? Or you want to shift your IRA from one institution to another. Go right ahead, but make sure you know the rules first.

The law allows for two types of IRA transfers. The first is known as a direct trustee-to-trustee transfer; the second is known as a rollover. Here's the difference.

In a trustee-to-trustee transfer, you never get your hands on your IRA funds. Instead, you direct the institution that maintains your IRA to send the funds in your account to a second institution, where you've set up another IRA.

You can transfer your IRA in this way as many times as you like during the year. Uncle Sam imposes no penalty.

Likewise, you won't be hit with a penalty if you shift funds from one investment vehicle to another within the same institution—again, as long as you never withdraw the money. In other words, if you maintain an IRA at a financial institution that offers a number of investment vehicles, you may shift funds from one vehicle to another—within that institution—as many times as you choose. You'll pay no penalty.

You should know, though, that shifting investment vehicles does present one potential problem. You might get slapped with a penalty that your financial institution imposes—the loss of two month's interest, for example, for withdrawing funds from a CD before its due date.

In some cases, when you shift investments in your IRA, the interest rate on the entire account may plunge to the lowest the financial institution is legally allowed to pay—usually passbook rates. Here's the reason: The bank or savings and loan regards the change as an early withdrawal—not simply a transfer of funds from one vehicle to another.

The rules are different for a rollover. In this case, you

IRA

actually withdraw your money from your IRA and deposit it in another IRA account. The key distinction: The money is, at least temporarily, in your possession.

Be careful: You have only 60 days to roll your money over into another IRA. If you miss the 60-day deadline, Uncle Sam will assume you've made a withdrawal and tax you currently on the amount. You'll also pay a 10-percent early-withdrawal penalty on the amount you've withdrawn.

Here's another important rule: You may withdraw your money and roll it over into another IRA account only once a year. If you do it more often—you guessed it—you'll pay a 10-percent early withdrawal penalty. In addition, you'll pay ordinary income taxes on the amount you take out.

Should you make a nondeductible contribution?

A question we're often asked is whether people should make nondeductible IRA contributions. As we saw, although Uncle Sam restricts tax deductible contributions to an IRA, he allows everyone to make nondeductible contributions of up to $2,000 a year.

Why make nondeductible contributions?

Earnings—interest, dividends, and appreciation—on

the dollars you set aside in an IRA build up at a faster rate than earnings on a regular savings account.

The reason is, you pay no taxes on these earnings until they're withdrawn, usually at retirement. In other words, you defer taxes on otherwise taxable income.

Sounds convincing, you say, but wait a minute. There are reasons not to make a nondeductible IRA contribution—among them, onerous record keeping requirements and penalties on withdrawals.

Should you need your money before you reach the age of fifty-nine and one-half, you'll most likely pay a 10-percent penalty on the part of your withdrawal that represents earnings on your nondeductible contribution. So you shouldn't use a nondeductible IRA to save for short-term goals. The early-withdrawal penalty may well negate the benefit of tax-deferred compounding.

One alternative we suggest to making a nondeductible IRA contribution is to invest in a tax-free bond or tax-free bond mutual fund. With tax-free bonds, you can often achieve similar results with your investment dollars—and face no restrictions.

This strategy isn't perfect either, though. You can get locked into bonds. With IRAs, you're free to invest your IRA dollars in any number of vehicles.

Also, the higher your tax bracket, the more attractive nondeductible contributions. Some people—and we are among them—bet that the 28 percent rate won't last. Finally, the longer you have until retirement, the more you'll benefit from a nondeductible IRA.

The following table shows the amounts you could accumulate *after paying taxes* if you invested $2,000 each year in a nondeductible IRA, a taxable CD, or a municipal bond fund over various periods of time. The table assumes a 28-percent tax rate.

Years to Retirement	*Nondeductible IRA 8%*	*CD 8%*	*Municipal Bond—6%*
10	$26,461	$26,066	$26,362
15	47,499	45,710	46,552
20	77,097	71,701	73,571
25	119,273	106,091	109,729
30	179,928	151,594	158,116

What's the bottom line? When it comes to making nondeductible IRA contributions, there's no right answer—and no wrong one, either. You must analyze your personal situation carefully and look at these key factors: your age, the length of time you have to retirement, the rates of return you can get on competing investments, and your federal and state tax rates.

IRAs can be a great way to save for retirement. But if you're self-employed, you have a better savings vehicle available to you: Keoghs. That's what we'll tell you about in our next chapter.

9

What You Need to Know About Keoghs

What nifty tax-saving device is available to most doctors, dentists, lawyers, plumbers, truck drivers, writers, actors, and moonlighters?

It's a Keogh plan, available to all self-employed people. Keoghs take their name from the late New York Congressman Eugene Keogh, author of the 1962 Self-Employed Individuals Retirement Act, the law that created the plans. And Keogh plans are what this chapter is all about.

TAX-SAVINGS KEOGHS

Here, we'll explain how to put your money into these terrific tax-favored plans.

Why did Congress create Keoghs?

Congress wanted those of you who are self-employed to have the same opportunity to save for retirement as people who are employed by someone else. In fact, nowadays the rules that apply to Keoghs don't differ much from the rules that apply to company-sponsored pension plans.

Why should you contribute to a Keogh?

Keoghs—like other tax-favored retirement vehicles—pack a one-two wallop. That is, you reduce your tax liability while saving for your golden years.

The dollars you sock away in a Keogh are deductible on your federal income tax return. Also, earnings on the dollars you put away build up tax deferred until they're withdrawn, usually at retirement.

Who is entitled to set up a Keogh?

Keoghs are designed for businesspeople and professionals who work for themselves. Some people think that only sole proprietors—meaning those who file Schedule Cs with their Form 1040s—are entitled to set up Keogh plans. They're wrong.

The law says that partnerships may establish Keoghs for their partners. Likewise, directors who serve on corporate boards and are paid for their services may set up Keoghs.

In short, Uncle Sam says that anyone with self-employment income—regardless of how little—is entitled to sock away dollars in a tax-favored Keogh plan.

How do Keoghs work?

You may not know it, but Keogh plans, like company-sponsored retirement plans, come in two types—defined-contribution plans and defined-benefit plans. With a defined-contribution plan, you set aside a specific amount of your earnings each year—10 percent, say. And the retirement benefit you receive is based not only on how much you put away but on how well the money was invested.

With a defined-benefit plan, you make annual contributions that are large enough to guarantee that you'll receive a specified amount each year after you retire.

How do defined-contribution plans for Keoghs work?

Defined-contribution plans themselves come in two types—profit-sharing plans and money purchase plans. Let's take a look at each.

When you set up a profit-sharing plan, Uncle Sam allows you to vary your contributions from year to year—a boon for small businesses that are strapped for cash.

Why? If your business isn't doing so well one year, Uncle Sam allows you—but doesn't require you—to make a contribution to your profit-sharing plan. So if you need the money for other purposes, it's available. You're not obligated to contribute to your plan.

The rules cap contributions to a profit-sharing plan at the lesser of $30,000 or 15 percent of your annual earnings. But this percentage is misleading.

The reason? The percentage is applied to your gross self-employment income *minus* your Keogh contribution. So, in effect, you may set aside only 13.042 percent of your net self-employment earnings for the year to a profit-sharing plan.

What about money purchase plans?

The ceiling on contributions to money purchase plans is the lesser of $30,000 or 25 percent of your gross self-employment earnings—again, less your contribution. So, effectively, you may contribute 20 percent of your self-employment earnings to a plan.

A money-purchase plan lets you contribute more toward your retirement nest egg than a profit-sharing plan, but it does have one disadvantage.

The rules require you to sock away a set percentage of your self-employment income each year, regardless of how profitable your business, or pay a penalty.

How much of a penalty? It comes to 10 percent of the amount you underfunded your plan. To make matters worse, if you don't pay the penalty in the time the IRS gives you, you'll receive a notice of deficiency from Uncle Sam. In that case, you'll be assessed 100 percent of the amount you underfunded.

What if you're not sure you can afford a 20-percent money purchase contribution each year? You can get around this problem by creating what's known as a paired plan, which is a combination of a money purchase plan and a profit-sharing plan. A paired plan gives you the best of both worlds.

You may still contribute as much as 20 percent to

your plan, but you aren't obligated to ante up the full amount from year to year.

Say you set up a paired plan. You use the money purchase portion of the plan to shelter a small percentage of your annual income—8 percent, say.

Then you use the profit-sharing portion of the plan to shelter any additional amounts you'd like to set aside. Though you must contribute at least 8 percent to the money-purchase plan, the amount you sock away in the profit-sharing plan is entirely up to you. That way, you may use your cash for other purposes if a problem crops up.

How do defined-benefit plans work?

Defined-benefit plans are more complex than defined-contribution plans. The plans promise to pay you a preset sum each year after you retire.

In 1990, the ceiling on yearly payouts from this type of plan comes to the lesser of $102,582 or—here's where it gets complicated—100 percent of your average annual earnings for the three consecutive years in which your earnings are the highest. (The ceiling is indexed annually for inflation.)

Say you decide it's time to call it quits. You resign

your post as a vice president for a big financial-services company and set up shop as a management consultant.

Your self-employment income adds up to $60,000 in 1988, $70,000 in 1989, and $80,000 in 1990. Now, you ask, how much may you set aside in a defined-benefit plan?

You may salt away enough to fund an annual retirement benefit of $70,000, which is your average earnings for those three consecutive years.

How much must you put away each year to fund a $70,000 pension? You'll need an actuary to calculate this amount, because the answer depends on your age, life expectancy, and the rate of return the dollars set aside in your Keogh will earn.

For example, someone who's fifty-five and plans to retire at age sixty-five must contribute more to fund a $70,000 retirement benefit than someone who's twenty-five. That's because the older person is funding the benefit over 10 years compared to 40 years for the younger person.

In fact, defined-benefit plans are ideal for anyone fifty years of age or older who has sizeable income to shelter from the long reach of Uncle Sam.

You should know, though, that the rules don't permit you to deduct in any single year a Keogh contribution that adds up to more than your earned income for that year. So your deductible contribution for 1990, say, couldn't equal more than $80,000, your earnings for that year.

You should also know that the $102,582 limit on retirement benefits from these plans is reduced if you hang up your hat before you reach the Social Security retirement age, which ranges from age sixty-five to sixty-seven, depending on the year you were born.

Your financial adviser will provide the details. One last point: We advise anyone even thinking about a defined-benefit plan to speak to a financial adviser first. These plans are complex and it's critical to set them up properly.

Where may you establish a Keogh?

The rules allow you to set up a Keogh at almost any financial institution—a bank, a brokerage firm, a mutual fund company, and so on.

When you establish a Keogh, you need an IRS-approved plan document. Most people set up Keoghs through master or prototype plans. These plans, which are already approved by the IRS, are offered by banks, brokerage houses, mutual funds, and many other financial-services companies.

You may also use a personalized or customized plan drawn up especially for you by a lawyer or pension plan expert. What's the advantage of such a plan?

It's flexible. Master or prototype plans may not have the features you need. For example, a prototype plan may not let you invest your Keogh dollars in real estate, say.

Also, a prototype plan from an institution may restrict you to investing your Keogh money in vehicles offered by that institution.

With a customized or self-directed plan, you're under no such limitations. For it, you simply set up a checking account—Jane Doe, Keogh, say—then purchase any investments you like.

In most cases, the cost of setting up a prototype Keogh is minimal, but a customized plan can cost you upwards of $500 in legal or consulting fees.

When you establish a Keogh, the rules require you to designate a trustee. Your financial institution may serve as the trustee of your Keogh plan, but so may you.

What's the deadline for setting up a Keogh?

Uncle Sam gives you until December 31 of each tax year to establish your Keogh plan. You don't have to deposit money in the plan when you set it up, but your Keogh must be in place by then—otherwise, no Keogh for you until the next tax year.

What's the deadline for funding a Keogh

The rules say you have until the due date of your tax return, including extensions, to fund your Keogh for the year.

Where may you invest your Keogh dollars?

Uncle Sam allows you to invest your Keogh dollars virtually anywhere—in certificates of deposit, stocks, bonds, mutual fund shares, even real estate.

But he says, if your Keogh is self directed, you may not put your Keogh money in art, antiques, collectibles, alcoholic beverages such as rare wines, or U.S. gold and silver coins. You may, however, place money in these investments if you have a trust or custodial account.

What happens if you use your Keogh dollars to purchase any of these prohibited items? The amount you've invested is treated as a withdrawal. That is, the amount is taxable as income to you, plus you pay a 10 percent penalty if you haven't reached age fifty-nine and one-half.

What if you miss the deadline for a Keogh?

You may still establish what's known as a simplified employee pension (SEP) plan. You don't have to set up your SEP until the due date of your Form 1040.

SEPs are popular because they're simple. To create one, all you need to do is fill out a form that's available at most financial institutions.

How do SEPs work?

A self-employed person establishes a SEP by creating an account in his or her name and contributing to it. What's the ceiling on deductible contributions to a SEP? It comes to 15 percent of your earnings, up to $30,000. Also, you shell out no taxes on the money deposited in your SEP. And—as with other plans—earnings that your SEP collects accumulate tax deferred until you withdraw your money.

Are there any other sources of retirement income? Indeed there are. In the next chapter, we'll take a look at some other options.

10

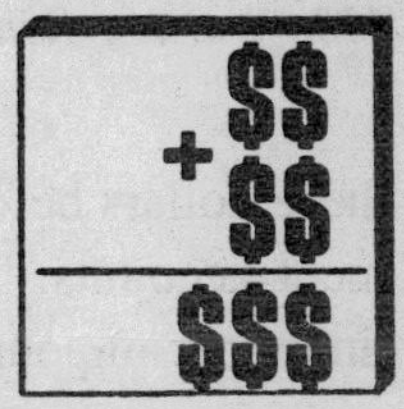

Your Other Sources of Retirement Income

You can sometimes tap into other sources of retirement income, besides the obvious ones—company-sponsored retirement plans and Social Security. What are your other potential sources? In this chapter, we take a look.

Do you have savings?

If you're like many people, you've saved dollars in addition to those deposited in your tax-favored retirement accounts. The money you've saved may come in handy once you retire. In fact, you may want to use these dollars before you withdraw cash from your retirement accounts. That way, your retirement dollars continue to compound tax-deferred.

Can you tap the equity in your house for cash?

Selling a house and moving to smaller quarters is a big step; one you need to consider carefully and discuss with your family. But some people do use the equity in their homes to provide extra retirement income. Let's run through how you'd project income from selling your house.

Say that you've just turned sixty-two, and you're an avid golfer. You've decided to sell your home and move to a condominium in North Carolina near a golf course. Your home is worth $300,000 today. The cost basis of your house—that is, its cost plus improvements—adds up to $80,000.

But Uncle Sam gives homeowners age fifty-five and older a big one-time tax break when they sell their principal residence. You may exclude from your taxable income the first $125,000 in capital gains that you realize from the sale.

Now let's assume neither you nor your spouse, if you're married, has used this tax benefit before, because if you had, you wouldn't qualify for this break again.

When we factor in the age 55 exclusion, the sale of your home looks like this:

Selling price	$ 300,000
Minus cost basis	(80,000)
Minus selling costs	(20,000)
Capital gain	$ 200,000

Now, we figure in the age 55 exclusion.

Capital gain	$ 200,000
Minus exclusion	(125,000)
Taxable gain on sale	75,000
Tax rate on gain	28 %
Taxes payable	$21,000

So, after giving Uncle Sam his due, you have the following funds left to invest:

Selling price	$ 300,000
Minus mortgage	0
Minus tax liability	(21,000)
Minus selling costs	(20,000)
Funds available	$ 259,000

If you invest the $259,000 and receive a return of 6 percent after tax, you'd add about $15,540 a year to your income. Not bad, you say, and you're right.

Of course, this amount wouldn't just be gravy. You'd still have housing costs. Say, though, you were able to purchase your North Carolina condominium for only $100,000. You would have $159,000 left over to invest. And while you would have maintenance expenses and taxes on your new condominium, they may be less than they were on your old house.

So, as you near retirement age—and, if you're not wedded to your house—you may want to evaluate the costs of other housing options, plus use some of the equity in your home to support your post-retirement lifestyle.

Can you tap your life insurance policy for cash?

Many people think of life insurance as something they'll never be around to enjoy. That's true of term life insurance, which provides only a death benefit.

But for dozens of other life insurance policies—whole life, universal life, single-premium life, and so on—nothing could be further from the truth.

Uncle Sam allows you to borrow the cash value of

your life insurance policy, although he imposes limits on how much you can take out.

You can also cancel your life insurance policy and get back its cash value, a useful option for people who want to supplement their retirement income and no longer need the coverage.

If you purchased your policy before June 21, 1988, you can borrow on your life insurance tax-free. What if you bought your policy after that date?

Another set of rules apply. In this case, if your life insurance premium payments top limits outlined by Uncle Sam, your policy will fall into the category of a modified endowment contract. And that's bad news for you tax-wise. Here's why.

With a modified endowment contract, Uncle Sam assumes that the first dollars you borrow or withdraw are your accumulated earnings. And these dollars are subject to federal income taxes.

Also, if you're under the age of fifty-nine and one-half, the IRS slaps you with a 10 percent penalty on the amount of earnings you borrow from such a plan. You may also be subject to a separate penalty in your state.

Now, what if your policy is classified as a modified endowment plan but you don't borrow or withdraw any of your dollars? Then it's business as usual.

The amounts you contribute to your policy continue to

accumulate tax-deferred until you withdraw them or assign or pledge the policy as collateral for a loan. When you assign or pledge a policy, the amount is treated as a distribution to you for tax purposes.

The modified endowment rules apply only to policies entered into or changed after June 20, 1988. And Uncle Sam exempts from these rules policies with death benefits of $25,000 or less that are purchased to cover burial expenses or in connection with prearranged funeral expenses. You should know though, that you must meet a number of conditions to qualify for this exemption. See your financial adviser for details.

Our advice?

If you want to avoid the tax trap of the modified endowment policy rules, see your tax adviser before you boost your premium payments. With the help of your insurance agent, he or she will be able to tell you if your plan will be reclassified as a modified endowment policy.

What about working after "retirement"?

Pensions and other retirement plans aren't the only way to get what you need for retirement. Another option is to work part time after you retire. You might even take on a second career.

One businessperson we know lectures on entrepreneurship at a local university. Another writes a column about real estate for a local newspaper.

Another idea: Start your own small business.

A longtime collector of Civil War memorabilia, for instance, set up shop as an antiques dealer after he took early retirement. Still another fulfilled her fantasy to run her own restaurant.

Working after retirement may not provide you with a lot of extra cash. For one, you must consider how your earnings will reduce your Social Security benefits. (See Chapter 20 for the rules.) But working does give most people a purposeful activity and a sense of self-worth—two benefits that can be more valuable than money.

Now you know about the sources that are available to you for retirement income. In the following chapters, we'll show you how you can make your investments pay off for your retirement years.

[illegible] people ... promotes home business opportunities [illegible] a local university. Another type of [illegible] small business ... [illegible]

Another idea: Start your own small business.

A [illegible] Civil War memorabilia, for instance, [illegible] can be a [illegible] into [illegible] [illegible]

[illegible] on a resolution.

[illegible] may not provide you with a [illegible] for [illegible] you must consider [illegible] Social Security [illegible] [illegible] benefits that can be more valuable than money.

[illegible] of the sources that are available to you [illegible]. In the following chapters, [illegible] you can [illegible] your retirement years [illegible] for your retirement years.

[illegible]

11

Fundamental Truths About Investing

There are so many things you can do as an intelligent investor that it makes sense to begin with a quick rundown of the taboos—things you don't want to do.

INVESTMENT STRATEGIES—THE DONT'S

You don't want to step into traps that have already snared countless investors. They've already paid the price. Learn from their experiences, and you won't have to. So let's spend just a little time here going over "strategies" that the well-prepared investor would do well to avoid. Keep in mind that when you invest with an eye toward retirement, you must avoid the same traps and employ the same strategies as you would for any successful investing.

Failing to properly analyze your current situation

If you learn only one lesson from this book, make it this one: Retirement planning is, in actuality, life planning. As we saw, our approach to retirement planning is built on finding the answers to three deceptively simple questions: What do you have? What do you want? How do you get what you want?

Once you know what you have and what you want, you're ready to develop investment strategies for every aspect of your retirement life.

As you develop these strategies, though, realize that what you don't want to do is take completely unnecessary risks when a lower-risk investment might get you where you need to go.

Likewise, you don't want to lock in an investment strategy. In retirement, your goals are constantly changing, so the same strategy isn't going to work for 20 years, say. You may want to travel for five years, for example, then provide for your grandchildren's college

education. As your goals change, your investment strategies should change.

Remember: Formulating goals doesn't stop with retirement. We all have goals and dreams we want to realize throughout our life.

Failing to think of the long term

You remember the crash of the stock market in October 1987. Say you sold your equities after the crash, then invested in CDs at eight percent. Believe it or not, you'd have less today than your fellow investor who held on to his or her equities.

Most people think of retirement as a short period of time. In the past it was, so retirees could comfortably invest in cash or fixed income. But no more. As we pointed out, today most people spend at least 20 years in retirement. So you need to think about—and invest—for the long term even during your retirement years.

Failing to understand investment categories

While you need to understand specific investments to be successful, you also need to understand investment categories.

You must understand how these categories perform

over the long term and how they perform in relation to each other. For example, many people have misconceptions about equities—they think that they're very risky and volatile. They can be—over a short period of time. However, if you look at their performance over the long haul, they're not that risky.

People also think that real estate always makes money. It doesn't. And most investors assume that bonds are steady and safe, while they're actually volatile.

The point we're trying to make here is that to understand an investment you must understand the investment categories and how they perform over the long term. We'll have more to say on this subject in later chapters.

Failing to diversify

Someone tells you stocks are the best place to invest your money, so you buy stocks. But then the market drops, and you've made no other investments that could cushion your loss. You failed to diversify.

In later chapters, we'll say a great deal more about how to diversify. It's not enough, as the situation above points out, to spread your investment dollars out within specific categories—common stocks, for instance. You must also diversify among categories in order to spread your risk.

Why is diversification so important? It protects you against a variety of risks, risks we'll describe fully in the next chapter.

Still not convinced? Here's a story that illustrates why diversification is so vital.

In early 1975 a man we'll call Ron wins $100,000 in a lottery. He decides to invest his windfall conservatively. Since 1973 and 1974 were terrible bear markets, he opts for purchasing long-term government bonds.

In 1979, interest rates sky rocket, and the value of his bonds plunges to $72,000. "Well," he decides, "I'm going to get out of the bond market and cut my losses." But what to do now? He remembers that gold was selling for $35 an ounce in 1972; today it's at $800 an ounce. Moreover, he just heard someone on the radio predict that gold would soar to $2,000 an ounce. So he decides to buy 90 ounces of gold with his $72,000.

Now the year is 1982, and gold has fallen to $300 an ounce. Ron has only $27,000 left of his lottery winnings, but this time he's going to be smart. In the early 1980s, he knows, the only investments that have performed well are oil and gas and real estate. As Ron sees it, only one investment makes sense. He decides to buy a condominium in Houston. He locates a $100,000 condominium, puts $27,000 down, and takes out a mortgage of $73,000.

The years pass and it's 1987. He's paid his mortgage down to $70,000, but Houston's real estate prices have crashed, and his condo is worth only $60,000. He now has a negative net worth of $10,000.

The moral of Ron's story: Diversify.

Trying to hit home runs

If your objective is to get to first base, a single is just as effective as a home run and a whole lot less risky. Make sure your investments fit your goals.

If, for instance, you reach a particular goal with a 7 percent annual return, which you can get with a reasonably safe certificate of deposit, that's a good enough investment for you. Why risk losing your capital just because another investment offers a potential 10 percent return?

Maybe you *like* to try for home runs occasionally. Then set aside a small portion of your funds for those kinds of long-shot investments.

Our rule of thumb: Decide what return you need to achieve your goal, and then risk only what's needed to get you there.

Relying on "hot tips"

Be wary of hot tips—from anyone. And be especially wary of casual tips from friends or acquaintances. The problem is that there's usually no way for you to check the value of the tip. The risk may be far higher than is prudent for you to accept.

Besides, it doesn't matter how great the source of the tip, by the time it gets to you, it's probably stone cold—even if there was something to it in the first place. Most investment professionals know that anybody can make money during certain favorable time periods. But that's not what counts. What enhances the return of individual investors over a long period of time is not losing money—or at least minimizing your losses. So keep the "don'ts" we just discussed in mind. They're the most effective way we know to keep losses to a minimum.

THE DO'S

Now that you know what not to do, let's take a look at the right way to build your nest egg for retirement—and keep it working for you during retirement.

Emphasize personal needs, not market or economic conditions

People pay too much attention to current market or economic conditions. As a result, they make short-term decisions. You must recognize, though, that as an individual investor, you're quite different from an institutional investor whose actions influence the market. The time horizon for most individuals is longer than for an institution. Retirement, for example, has quite a long time horizon.

Institutional investors are under short-term pressure to perform. They try to outguess other institutional investors and the market. And they do it 80 hours a week. Most individuals don't have that kind of time to spend focusing on their investments—nor do they want to.

You, as an individual, need to look at your investments in relation to your goals, not in relation to what's happening today in the market. In other words, you must be fully aware of your internal concerns, not just external conditions. If you invest solely on the basis of changing market conditions, you'll probably make serious mistakes. But if you invest with your goals and objectives in mind, you can usually ignore short-term market fluctuations.

Focus equally on risk and return

Investment advisers who also sell investment products have a direct interest in underplaying the element of risk. To dwell on this unpleasant aspect of any investment discourages product sales. So they prefer to talk about potential returns. But a smart investor makes risk assessment as important as return.

The biggest risk an individual investor faces is losing money. When people speak about risk, they often do so abstractly. They talk, for example, of taking the risk of crossing the street before the light turns. However, you need to think more concretely about risk. You need to ask yourself how much of your money you can afford to lose in any one year.

Individuals are risk averse—they don't like losing money. But you can't obtain a positive return after taxes and inflation if you don't take some risk. If you stick only with ultrasafe Treasury notes, say, you'll never beat inflation over the long term after you subtract what you owe Uncle Sam.

So even though you're loss-averse, you must take some risk to beat inflation. It's a tradeoff—but a necessary one.

Focus on real rate of return

Inflation and income taxes dramatically reduce your rate of return on your investments. That's why we focus on your "real rate of return."

How do you calculate your real return? Figure your after-tax rate of return, then subtract the current rate of inflation. The result is your real rate of return.

Say you invest in a bond yielding an after-tax rate of return of 5 percent. If inflation is running at 4 percent a year, your real rate of return is 1 percent. What if inflation jumps to 12 percent a year? Your investment is actually declining in value by 7 percent a year.

Here's another example. Say you're currently earning 8 percent on a money-market fund. Here's how you figure your real rate of return:

gross return		8 %
federal and state tax rate	30%	
after-tax rate of return (8% less [8% times 30%])		5.6%
inflation		(4 %)
real rate of return (5.6% minus 4%)		1.6%

Now let's contrast this scenario with the early 1980s

when money-market accounts were earning 18 percent. As you can see, the picture is quite different.

gross return		18%
federal and state tax rate	50%	
after-tax rate of return (18% less [18% times 50 percent])		9%
inflation		(12%)
real rate of return		(3%)

By keeping focused on your real rate of return, you can calculate if your investments are staying ahead of inflation. Keep in mind: Investment experts point out that a 1 percent to 4 percent real rate of return is a significant accomplishment.

Seek to preserve capital while creating wealth

Let's say that you're seventy years old, retired, comfortably wealthy, and play lots of golf. Obviously, your investment goal is to preserve the nest egg you have, and your investment strategies should involve little risk. What, after all, could a risky investment get you that you don't already have?

On the other hand, suppose that you're twenty-five

years old. You have no family, few assets, and great professional prospects. You have no capital to preserve, so your goals all relate to creating wealth. And, because you have plenty of time until you retire, your investment strategies can—and probably should—involve a relatively high degree of risk.

Most of us, though, find ourselves somewhere between these two extremes. We can't afford to put all our capital at risk, but we certainly need to build more wealth. Helping you achieve the right balance for your retirement strategy is one of the aims of this book.

Our strategy, then, is to show you how you can obtain a positive real rate of return with a minimum amount of risk. When you create a positive real rate of return, you're creating real wealth—even if that real rate of return is only 1 percent to 4 percent.

Seek to diversify investments

The old caveat about not putting all your eggs in a single basket remains true. Even the "best" investment shouldn't be your only investment. Every investor looking toward retirement needs to diversify in order to control his or her level of risk.

And risk is what the next chapter is all about.

12

The Realities of Risk

Sure, you know that any investment is risky, that there's some chance of losing all or some of your money. And like most investors, you are—naturally enough—averse to losing money. You wouldn't be human if you weren't. However, you should also know that you need to earn a positive real rate of return. And you can't do it, unles you take some risk.

So in this chapter, we'll tell you about the risks of investing. As you'll see, we break risk down into six categories. In the next chapter, we'll show you how to minimize those risks.

What is inflation risk?

Put simply, inflation risk is the fact that the dollars you earn on your investments each year buy less and less. And this fact is bad news for people in retirement. Not surprisingly, a Merrill Lynch survey points out that what retirees fear most is inflation. The reason? Many people in retirement live on fixed incomes, and inflation can wreak havoc on their purchasing power.

Another way of looking at inflation risk: If the inflation rate goes up, the value of investments that you currently hold may go down.

Inflation *per se*, even a high rate of inflation, is not risky in the sense that we're speaking of risk. When you buy a bond or any debt instrument, the price you pay already reflects the underlying inflation rate—whether it's high or low.

What you risk is an increase in the inflation rate, a change in the rate at which the currency is devaluating. If you buy a bond and the inflation rate rises, the interest it pays will buy less and less.

What is interest rate risk?

As inflation goes up, so do interest rates. And, as interest rates rise, the value of certain investments, bonds for example, drop. (Alternatively, when rates drop, the value of bonds rises.) Here's the reason: To keep up with market rates, issuers of bonds and other fixed-income instruments have to pay higher rates on their new issues when interest rates go up. So older issues, paying lower rates of interest, are worth less.

In other words, an increase in the interest rate paid on some particular debt instrument—five-year corporate bonds, for instance—has the effect of lowering the value of existing debt instruments previously issued at lower rates. The 7 percent, five-year bond you bought last year would fall in value if similar bonds issued this year paid 9 percent.

What is deflation risk?

Deflation risk refers to the possibility that the value of an investment may fall as general price levels drop during economic depression or severe recession. A house that you bought in boom times, for example, may not fetch the same price when unemployment is high.

What is business risk?

Business risk is the specific risk associated with the underlying business of a particular stock, bond, or other investment. It's the risk that some event, probably unforeseen, may reduce the return on a particular investment. If, for instance, you've invested in a company that makes a popular cold remedy, and somebody comes up with a sure-fire cure for the common cold, your company's product suddenly isn't worth much. The value of your investment declines.

Another example of business risk: A company that is unable to make a bond payment.

What is market risk?

The best example of market risk? The stock market crash of 1987 when the value of stocks of rock-solid companies plunged with all other stocks. Market risk, then, is the danger that whole financial markets can rise or decline in value. As they do, they may affect the value of a particular investment in the market, even though the other risk factors for that investment remain unchanged.

When stock market investors, for instance, get nervous, the general value of all stocks is likely to fall—your stock in General Widget Corp. included, even though the prospects for widget sales remain high.

A new tax law, the imposition of a new regulation, civil unrest in a Third World country that supplies some vital raw material, or a spell of particularly bad weather—any unexpected change—can adversely affect the entire market—and the value of one or more of your investments.

What is illiquidity risk?

Most investments are liquid. You call your broker, say you want to sell some investment, sell it, and pocket your money. Some investments, though, aren't quite as liquid—real estate or stock in a private company, for example. When you own one of these less liquid investments, you either must wait to sell or take a substantial discount if you sell immediately.

Suppose you have to sell one of these investments before you had planned. Maybe you've incurred an unexpected expense, a large medical bill, for instance. When you are forced to sell, you must take what the market offers at the time. You don't have the option of waiting for a better price. That's illiquidity risk.

Do investments involve more than one kind of risk?

You bet they do. Investments often involve all six types of risk to one degree or another. But the categories of risk have varying effects on different investments. Some investments are affected more than others by certain types of risk. For example, real estate is especially sensitive to illiquidity risk and bonds to interest-rate risk.

What kinds of risks should you accept?

A cynic might say that managing risk is easy. You need only to know whether the inflation rate and interest rates are going up or down, then shift your investments to match these forecasts. The fact is, if you could predict with accuracy, you would be successful.

However, as many of us in the financial services industry have observed, people who try to determine market changes—often called "market timers"—don't consistently make the right call and studies have shown that the market timing approach works only if you make the right call two-thirds of the time or more. Even the experts have trouble meeting this challenging target consistently.

Moreover, as we noted, most people are loss-averse. They can't afford to take substantial risks with their savings. That's why we believe that the goal of an investment strategy should be to preserve purchasing power and create value while minimizing the impact of risk. We'll explain in the next chapter.

13

What You Need to Know About Asset Allocation

If you're like most people investing for retirement, you believe that which stocks you buy—or which bonds or which commodities—determine how successfully you'll build a nest egg for the future. But this belief is another one of those stubborn myths. "Determinants of Portfolio Performance," a study that appeared in the July-August 1986 Financial Analysts Journal, showed that less than 6 percent of the total return on your investments depends upon the specific investments that you make. The authors of the study looked at 10 years of investment performance—from 1974 to 1983—of 91 large corporate pension plans and considered three key decisions made by those plans: asset classes, timing, and security selection.

Far more important to your investment performance, they concluded, is how you allocate or spread your investment dollars among four different categories of assets:

- Cash and cash equivalents
- Fixed income instruments
- Equities
- Hard assets

The research shows that as much as 94 percent of your investment return—maybe even more—depends upon your allocation of funds to these categories.

And asset allocation is critical whether you're in your twenties or thirties and trying to sock away money for retirement or in your sixties or seventies and already enjoying your leisure years.

There's nothing complicated about the concept of asset allocation. Simple stated, put some amount in each category. The question, of course, is how much? How do you decide what proportion of your funds to invest in the different categories? What facts do you need to know?

That's what this chapter is all about. You need a lot of

information if you're going to allocate your investment dollars wisely—and profitably. And, of course, you must allocate your resources quite differently depending on your age and your future goals.

First, we'll tell you what kind of information you need. Then, we'll explain how to evaluate it, and, finally, where you go from there.

As you read through this chapter, keep in mind that an allocation strategy for retirement is only the final result of a process in which you evaluate and consider the relationship of risk and return and the need for diversification.

These two concepts are fundamental to the success of your retirement asset allocation strategy. So we'll review and expand upon them in the pages that follow.

How do you manage risk and return?

It's axiomatic that the greater the return you expect to achieve with any investment, the greater the risk you must be prepared to take.

If that weren't true, no one would make high-risk investments. So take a look at the table below. It lists the average returns for the most common types of investments—from stocks and bonds to government securities—for a one-year holding period.

Asset	*Average Fluctuation*	*return plus or minus**
Common stocks	12.1%	41.8
Long-term corporate bonds	5.3%	16.8
Long-term government bonds	4.7%	17.0
U.S. treasury bills	3.6%	6.6
Inflation	3.2%	9.6

Source: Ibbotson Associates based on actual returns from 1926 to 1988

* 95 percent of the return varied around the average by plus or minus the percentage shown.

The returns in this table are averages over a one-year holding period.

As you can see, the table shows that as the risk of an investment rises, so, too, does the possibility of a much smaller return—even a loss. For example, the average return for company stocks, was 12.1 percent, but you could have pocketed a return as high as 53.9, (12.1 plus 41.8) or as low as negative 29.7 (-41.8 less 12.1).

In other words, choosing high-risk investments doesn't guarantee high returns. If it did, everyone would naturally make high-risk investments.

What effect does your time horizon have on managing risk?

We said that the returns in the table above represent averages over a one-year holding period. But what would happen if we expanded the return to say, 10 years—a period which could match the amount of time you have to save for retirement.

The next chart illustrates the range of returns you can expect with investments over various time periods. As you can see your risk decreases substantially over time. If you look at common stocks, say, over one year and ten years, the average return is the same, but the volatility decreases dramatically. So by investing over a long time horizon, you're lowering your risk considerably.

How else do you balance return and risk?

If you can't eliminate risk—and no one has yet discovered how—you can at least minimize it. That's the purpose of diversifying your investments, and there are two ways of going about it.

First, you remember, you want to lower your risk by spreading your investment dollars among different categories of investments. At the same time, you want to make sure that your dollars are diversified within the same investment category.

Let's look at diversification among investment categories first. Say you're in your forties and buy shares in a mutual fund that invests only in fast-growing companies. Aware of the need to diversify, you also buy a

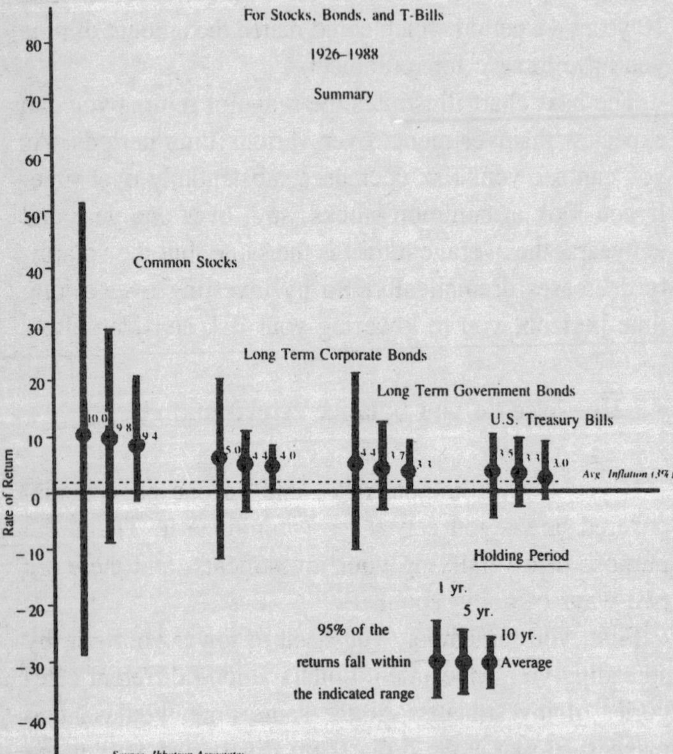
Range of Annual Returns
For Stocks, Bonds, and T-Bills
1926–1988
Summary
80
70
60
50
40
30
20
10
0
-10
-20
-30
-40
Rate of Return
Common Stocks
Long Term Corporate Bonds
Long Term Government Bonds
U.S. Treasury Bills
10.0
9.8
9.4
5.0
4.4
4.0
4.4
3.7
3.5
3.0
Avg. Inflation (3%)
Holding Period
1 yr.
5 yr.
10 yr.
Average
95% of the
returns fall within
the indicated range
Source: Ibbotson Associates

long-term corporate bond. How have these investments helped to minimize your risk? How will they help you reach your goal of building a solid retirement nest egg?

Well, if inflation should go up, so will the value of your mutual fund. On the other hand, a prolonged recession would probably drive down the value of your mutual fund shares.

The respective effects on the value of your corporate bond, however, would be exactly reversed. Higher inflation means your bond is worth less. Lower inflation, or a general decline in the price level, improves both the resale value and the income value of your bond.

The negative effects of a rising inflation rate on one of your investments is offset by the positive effects on the other. You've reduced your inflation risk—and increased your chances of building retirement dollars—by diversifying among investment categories. How do different categories of investments respond to inflation? You'll find the answer in the chart that follows.

Take another look at the fixed income category in the chart. As you can see, this category performs very well during periods of deflation, but poorly in periods of excessive inflation. If you look at the tangible category, however, you see that in periods of deflation it performs poorly, but in inflationary periods it does very well.

INFLATION AND ASSET CATEGORY BEHAVIOR INFLATION SCENARIO

Asset Category	Deflation (>.5%<0%)	Low (>0%%<3%)	Moderate (>3%<6%)	High (>6%<12%)	Excessive (>12%<20%)
Cash Equivalents	F	F	F	F	F
Fixed Income	E	G	G	P	P
Equities	P	E	G	F	P
Natural Resources	P	F	F	G	E
Real Estate	P	F	G	E	P
Tangibles	P	P	F	G	E

Asset Behavior Legend:

E=EXCELLENT (Substantial REAL Rate of Return)
G=GOOD (Reasonable REAL Rate of Return)
F=FAIR (Tend to track rate of inflation)
P=POOR (Loss of purchasing power)

James L. Joslin, Suzanne G. Lorant and Robert E.C. Werner
The Multi-Asset Allocation Model; A Financial Planning Framework for
Long-Term Investment Management. Tax Management Financial Planning Journal Vol. 2, NO.21 Oct 1986

How else do you diversify?

You also need to diversify within investment categories—especially in common stocks and in real estate. The more different stocks you own, for instance, the less vulnerable you are to the business risk associated with any single stock. Owning several parcels of real estate shields you from the risk of disaster—fire, for instance, or perhaps a change in freeway plans that alters the value of your property—that might affect just one parcel.

These, then, are the basic elements of asset allocation: risk, return, and diversification. Now we'll show you how to put these basics to work in building an intelligent investment retirement strategy through asset allocation.

What do you need to know about allocation?

Individuals—depending upon how long they intend to invest, their tolerance for risk, and how much they have to invest—should allocate their assets differently. We'll cover those individual choices.

But before we can do that intelligently, we have to lay out the basic principles of asset allocation. These are the tools you'll use when you get around to building your own investment strategy.

Anyone thinking about allocating assets will be asking

two simple but fundamental questions: Among which investment categories should I be allocating my resources, and which resources should I be allocating?

You may not believe it, but no matter how cluttered the investment marketplace seems to be with fancy new products, there are really only four investment categories. As we saw earlier, the four are: cash and cash equivalents, such as money-market funds, checking accounts, and short-term certificates of deposit; fixed-income vehicles, a group that includes tax-exempt bonds, corporate bonds, mortgages, and long-term certificates of deposit; equities, including both domestic and international stocks; and hard assets, such as real estate, gold, silver, oil, and natural gas.

Within these categories there are, of course, wide variations. Utility stocks, for instance, don't behave much like the stocks of young, high-tech or biotechnology companies. Utility stocks are much less volatile than high-tech or biotechnology stocks. You'll have to take these variations into account when you make your specific investment choices.

One other point: Because real estate, natural resources, and tangible assets usually move up or down in value together, it makes more sense to lump them into a single category, which we call "hard assets." Keep in mind, though, that not all hard assets are alike.

Real estate is traditionally less risky than natural resources or tangibles, but you may have some special knowledge of natural resources that gives you an advantage over other investors. The point is that though we lump them together, hard assets aren't really the same for all people.

What resources should I be allocating?

We often hear this question raised and as you can imagine, there are many different opinions. Basically, the question is should I look at all of my investments and develop a broad allocation strategy—or should I put my investments in individual pots related to individual goals? We recommend the former, with letting the latter (your goals) influence the allocation. We will say more on this later. What goes into the pile to be allocated—IRA funds, 401(k) funds, monies set aside for children's education?

All of it. Any investment which is "movable" should be included. A frequent question we are asked is whether equity in your home or vacation property should be included. Unless you are in a position to sell the property and invest the funds elsewhere, leave it out.

How does diversification work?

You're almost ready to start building your own diversification strategy—but not quite yet.

We've outlined the four categories of investments among which you can diversify. We've discussed which assets should be included in your diversification plans. Next we'll show you how, in general, to approach diversification. Then, in Chapter 19, you'll be able to apply these basic diversification principles to your own, individual financial situation and retirement circumstances.

For now, though, we'll ignore your personal circumstances and construct a diversification model that assumes a moderate, steady level of inflation. We'll also put an equal amount in each asset category, though we'll modify these amounts shortly.

Before we begin, though, you might be interested in the results of a study of the benefits of diversification done by Bailard, Biehl & Kaiser, an investment management firm in San Francisco. The study showed that even a naive approach to diversification—that is, investing equally in asset categories—was effective in preventing a loss in any single year.

The investment firm used five asset categories, rather than four, but the principle is exactly the same as the one we've outlined. The five investments were Treasury bills (cash and cash equivalents), government bonds (fixed income), New York Stock Exchange issues (equities), international securities (foreign bonds and equities), and real estate (hard assets).

The firm hypothetically invested 20 percent in each of these categories. At the end of every year, it reduced the amount in the winning asset categories and purchased more in the losing categories in order to keep a 20-percent mix in each category.

In the 38-year period covered by the study, equities had eight down years. But when the firm balanced these losses against gains in the other asset categories, the result was an overall loss in only two years.

As the following graph illustrates for the most recent 19 years, the volatility that many individual investors find so unnerving was greatly reduced by simply diversifying among classes of investments.

Now, on to our model.

With our four categories, an equal division of assets looks like this:

Cash and cash equivalents	25%
Fixed-income vehicles	25
Equities	25
Hard assets	25
	100%

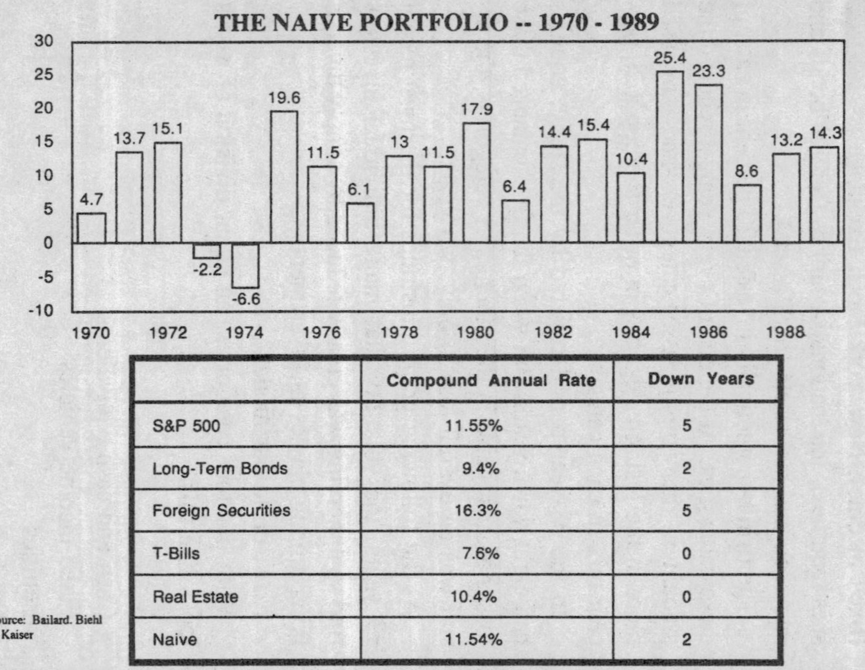

	Compound Annual Rate	Down Years
S&P 500	11.55%	5
Long-Term Bonds	9.4%	2
Foreign Securities	16.3%	5
T-Bills	7.6%	0
Real Estate	10.4%	0
Naive	11.54%	2

Source: Bailard. Biehl & Kaiser

But it isn't wise to give cash equal treatment when allocating your resources, because, in most cases, an investment in cash is short term. It's not where you want to keep your money. You've only parked it there for liquidity or while waiting for a more profitable investment opportunity.

So, under normal circumstances, you wouldn't want to keep 25 percent of your assets in cash, especially since the value of cash is inexorably whittled away by inflation. Let's reduce that proportion of your assets allocated to cash to something more reasonable.

Cash and cash equivalents	10%
Fixed-income vehicles	30
Equities	30
Hard assets	30
	100%

As far as cash is concerned, you've now minimized the undermining effects that a steady inflation rate has on its value. But what about changes in the inflation rate? Variations in the inflation rate don't have much effect on the value of cash. But they do influence the value of other securities. What should you do, in general, about that situation?

Equities don't all behave the same. For instance,

whether a particular stock moves in the direction of inflation depends on the industry in which the company operates and the company itself.

Fixed-income securities, usually, are a hedge against deflation. Hard assets are a hedge against inflation. However, you want to minimize hard assets as well, because of the risk and illiquidity.

So what are some strategies for minimizing risk?

Minimizing different kinds of risk takes different strategies. To minimize market risk, you should diversify among the four asset categories, then allocate your equity category further among stocks with varying degrees of risk—for example, 20 percent aggressive growth stocks, 35 percent growth stocks, and 45 percent growth-and-income stocks.

What about the risk of inflation or deflation? Diversifying and allocating assets among the four asset categories should minimize the risk from both these directions.

To reduce interest rate risk, you should stagger the maturities of your fixed-income investments, so they come due at different times. That way, you won't be taking as much a chance on interest rates.

Say you want to allocate $100,000 of your portfolio to

bonds. To stagger your maturities, you might take 40 percent of your $100,000, or $40,000, and buy 5 intermediate bonds—that is, bonds maturing in three to seven years.

So you would purchase five $8,000 bonds that are slated to mature in three, four, five, six, and seven years. Sixty percent of your $100,000 you would allocate to long-term bonds—those maturing in more than seven years. So you might buy three separate $20,000 bonds, maturing in eight, nine, and ten years.

You can minimize business risk by diversifying among the four asset categories and by using mutual funds.

Finally, you can reduce liquidity risk by allocating to the cash and cash equivalent category enough money to maintain sufficient reserves or rely on credit lines to meet your normal and unexpected needs. That way you won't be forced to sell bonds, equities, or real estate at a time when the market doesn't favor them.

What's next?

As we saw, you can reduce risk by expanding your time horizon—that is, investing for the long term. In the next four chapters, we'll look more closely at the four asset allocation categories. We'll see in the following chapter how you can use mutual funds. Then, in Chapter 19, you'll learn how to build your own portfolio to guarantee a secure retirement for you and your family.

14

All About Cash and Cash Equivalents

Everybody knows what cash is, but cash equivalents? What are those? And what characteristics do cash and cash equivalents bring to your diversified investment portfolio both before and after you retire?

In this chapter, we'll cover the cash category's special qualities that have a practical impact on your investment decisions—while you're still working and after you reach retirement age.

Cash equivalents offer investors liquidity and safety. Dollars invested in these vehicles won't fluctuate in value. Also, many cash investments, such as short-term certificates of deposit (CDs), carry no transaction costs—meaning there are no sales commissions or management fees to pay. And, cash investments can be as convenient as your corner bank or savings and loan.

In this chapter, we'll also outline the different kinds of taxable and nontaxable cash-equivalent investments available to you.

What about money-market accounts?

Don't confuse money-market accounts, offered by banks and savings and loans, with money-market funds, offered by brokerage houses and mutual fund companies. There are a number of differences. Think of money-market accounts as limited checking accounts—you can write only a few checks a month—that pay interest. The rate of interest varies, usually in some relation to market rates. But banks and savings and loans that offer money-market accounts aren't bound by law to tie their interest rates to any market indicator. They may vary them as often and as much as they like.

The best part of a money-market account is that you can pull your cash out immediately, any time you like, with no penalty involved. That's something you can't do with a CD, as we'll see. And that's one reason money-market accounts are good places to maintain an emergency fund. Moreover, your principal and interest—up to $100,000—are guaranteed by the federal government as long as your account is in an institution that's a member of the Federal Deposit Insurance Corporation (FDIC) or the National Credit Union Administration (NCUA).

However, money you deposit in a bank and at one of its branches aren't insured separately by Uncle Sam. They're treated as deposits at the same bank.

Here's something else you may not know. Uncle Sam insures each account separately as long as you maintain the account in different names. For example, you could have three accounts—one in your name, one in your spouse's name, and one in both your names—and each account would be insured up to $100,000.

But money-market accounts have their drawbacks, too. Unlike CDs, which as we'll see guarantee you a fixed rate of interest until maturity, money-market accounts give you no such guarantee. Furthermore, the interest rate paid on money-market accounts is usually lower than on CDs. (Sometimes, you can get the same or higher rate, though, if you select a money-market account with a high minimum deposit.)

So you don't want to tie up too much money in these accounts, particularly if you are already retired and want to know for certain what your income will be each month. We recommend that most people keep no more than three month's living expenses in a money-market account for emergencies.

When comparing money-market accounts at different banks you'll want to check the soundness of the institution as well as the yield it offers. In other words, to make sure you're getting a good return look for an institution that's likely to be in business for years to come and that offers competitive rates.

What else should you ask when you're comparing money-market accounts? You'll also want to ask about minimum balances required, the charge (if any) for each check you write, and other rules limiting your flexibility.

What about money-market funds?

Unlike money-market accounts, money-market funds are not insured by a state or government agency. But that shouldn't cause you much concern, as we'll explain later in this chapter. And the funds usually pay a higher rate of interest than bank money-market accounts.

Money-market funds do have some of the same features as checking accounts. If you intend to use one as a checking account, however, you'll want to carefully research the restrictions the fund imposes. Many, but not all, specify a minimum deposit (often $100) and withdrawal amount ($250 or $500).

Unlike other mutual funds, the share value in a money-market fund remains fixed at $1.00. Say you invest $2,000. You'll own 2,000 shares. Dividends are paid as shares. If the fund earns 8 percent and you let your dividends accumulate, at the end of a year you'll own 2,160 shares.

Money-market funds come in three varieties determined by the types of securities in which the funds usually invest.

General-purpose funds buy a wide variety of securities, including short-term government bills, corporate notes and certificates of deposit. Even the nongovernment debt, however, carries extremely low risk, and general-purpose money-market funds are not considered risky investments by the most conservative of investors.

Other funds specialize. Government funds invest only in securities issued by the federal government, so these funds offer the highest level of safety to the fund owners. Again, if you're already retired, you might think this extra protection is worth the slightly lower yield. If this added protection is of concern to you, however, make sure that the fund actually invests in government securities, not in repurchase agreements that are just backed by government securities. These funds don't offer the same degree of safety.

One other advantage of Government funds is that your

earnings are usually exempt from state income taxes, although they are taxable on your federal return.

The third type of fund is nontaxable. It invests only in obligations of state and local governments that are exempt from federal taxation. Tax-free funds pay dividends at a lower rate than the other two types. But, of course, your earnings are not reduced by taxes.

Are tax-exempt funds free from state and local taxes? The answer depends on how the fund invests its dollars. Funds that invest in obligations issued within your home state are usually exempt from these taxes.

You can find substantial differences—as much as a percentage point—in the dividend rates even among funds of the same type. Fund managers differ in how well they do their jobs. You'll want to shop around for the fund with the highest consistent yield over the last, say, 6 to 12 months.

What do you need to know about CDs?

When you put your money in a CD, you're allowing a bank or other institution to have the use of your cash for a specified period of time. In return for your doing so, the bank pays you interest.

Uncle Sam allows banks and savings institutions to

offer certificates of deposit at whatever amount, maturity, and interest rate they choose. This means that you can shop among banks—and increasingly at full-service or discount brokerage firms—to find the CD package that's best for your current needs.

Interest rates on CDs do vary, so don't assume that you can't do better than the bank on the corner. Since you can buy and redeem CDs by mail, it's just as easy to do business with a bank in another state as with the one across the street.

You should know that, as with money-market funds and accounts, comparing the interest rate on CDs offering similar rates and maturity can be a bit tricky. Again, It's not really the interest rate you care about, but the yield. Two CDs might pay the same rate of interest, but if interest on the second is compounded more frequently than on the first—daily instead of monthly, say—the yield on the second CD will be higher. In effect, you're earning more interest on your interest.

So when comparing certificates, always ask about yield.

Also, a couple of caveats are in order. First, if the interest rates a bank offers is substantially higher than the going rate for CDs of similar size and maturity, be skeptical. Maybe the bank is terribly short of funds or in a shaky financial situation and must offer the higher rate to attract new money. Yes, if the bank is an FDIC institution, FDIC insurance would cover your loss if the bank went belly up, but not necessarily the interest that is due you. Also, your money could be tied up for weeks or even months. This possibility is particularly distressing if you rely on your bank CD for income every month.

A second warning: CDs with maturities longer than two years are more like bonds than cash equivalent investments.

With the longer-term CDs, you face more risk from fluctuation in inflation and interest rates. If you buy a five-year certificate, for instance, and market rates rise substantially in the second year, you won't be able to take advantage of the higher rates.

And that's a third item to check. When buying a CD, make sure to find out about early withdrawal provisions and penalties. In some cases, a bank or savings and loan can slap you with a penalty that totals the entire amount of interest that's due you.

Here's another tip. You can purchase CDs from brokerage firms, as well as from banks and thrifts. And it might be advantageous for you to do so. You'll pay a brokerage fee, of course, but brokerage houses often pay a higher rate of interest on the certificates. The reason:

They buy these instruments in large quantities from banks, so they can frequently negotiate a higher rate.

Moreover, you may not be hit with a penalty if you withdraw your CD before its due date from a brokerage firm. That's because brokerages make what's known as a secondary market in CDs. That means if you want to redeem your CD early, there's no problem. The broker just sells your certificate to some other investor.

Here's another idea if you want to defer interest income on your CDs from one year to the next. Simply purchase a certificate that matures the following year. The IRS will tax your earnings when your CD comes due.

You should know that you can defer taxes in this way only on certificates that mature in one year or less. If you invest in a CD that has a longer maturity, Uncle Sam says you must report the amount of interest you accrue each year, even if you don't see the cash until your certificate matures.

Often, too, banks give you a choice of when you can receive interest. So if you want to defer paying taxes on your earnings, ask the bank about their rules.

Here's another point you should know. Most banks or other financial institutions won't let you cash just part of a CD. You must withdraw all your money—or none.

However, many banks let you withdraw interest you earn at any time during the term of the CD.

Are U.S. Treasury securities right for you?

Treasury bills, T-bills as they're usually called, are short-term obligations of the United States government that mature in one year or less. Since they're backed by the full faith and credit of the United States government, there's no safer place for your principal, which is why they're favored both by retirees and younger folks who want at least a portion of their money socked away in ultrasafe instruments.

There's a hitch, though. You must buy T-bills in denominations of $10,000 and higher—and thereafter in multiples of $5,000. T-Bills mature in 90 days, 180 days, or 52 weeks.

Your T-bill earnings are taxable at the federal level, but they're exempt from all state and local taxes. So if you live in a high tax state, such as California, Massachusetts, or New York, Treasury securities may be especially attractive to you.

Here's another advantage to buying a T-bill. It couldn't be easier to defer all the interest you earn to the following tax year. Simply buy a bill that comes due the following year. (This strategy, however, works only for

T-bills—that is, for government obligations with maturities of one year or less.

Many people, especially if they're retired, worry that they might need their cash before the year is up. But that's not much of a problem. T-bills are completely liquid. You can sell them through a broker at any time. But when you sell a bill before its maturity, you may realize a gain or loss, depending on whether current interest rates are lower or higher than the rate in effect when you bought the bill.

Where do you buy T-bills?

You can purchase them through a broker or bank, both of which charge small commissions—usually $25 to $50 per transaction. These commissions, of course, reduce your return.

You can eliminate this charge by buying T-bills directly from a Federal Reserve Bank. The 12 Federal Reserve Banks, acting as agents for the Treasury Department, sell U.S. government obligations to the public with no sales commissions.

If you telephone the Federal Reserve Bank nearest you or write the Bureau of Public Debt, Department F, Washington, DC 20239-1200, you can receive a free brochure on how to buy Treasury securities from a Federal Reserve Bank.

How do you decide which cash equivalent is right for you?

The answer depends on what matters most to you—safety, liquidity, saving taxes, convenience, or return. Investing in cash equivalents is a function of tradeoffs. For example, with T-bills, you get a high degree of safety but a lower return. With a money-market fund, you get liquidity but less safety. With bank CDs, you get convenience and a higher return, but less liquidity.

Now that you know about cash and cash equivalents, we'll take a look in the next chapter at our second investment category: fixed-income securities.

15

Fixed Income Investments

Like cash, bonds and other fixed-income securities have their special functions in a properly diversified investment portfolio. And they've always played a special role in a retirement portfolio. Fixed income instruments, however, aren't what they used to be.

In our grandparent's day, they were staid, stable, and even boring—and, for that reason, favored by both retirees and those wanting to invest a portion of their retirement funds in "reliable" securities. But that's no longer the case.

Today, fixed-income securities can be as varied and as volatile as any of your investments. In fact, most people don't know it, but from March to October of 1987—

before the heartstopping 1987 crash in the stock market—bonds lost from 10 to 25 percent of their value depending on their term and quality.

The fact that fixed income securities can be volatile, however, doesn't mean that they aren't good investments. Most people who are either looking toward retirement or already retired should include bonds and other fixed-income investments in their portfolios because they offer a steady flow of income and often an attractive rate of return.

So, you ask, what do you need to know to invest wisely in bonds and other fixed-income securities? In a minute, we'll take a look, but first we'll cover a few basics.

What do you need to know about bonds?

The most important point to remember about bonds is this: Interest rates and bond prices are inextricably intertwined. When interest rates fall, the value of bonds rise. When rates rise, the value of your bonds drop.

But what, you may ask, is a bond?

It's nothing more than a contract between the issuer of the bond, the borrower, and the person who holds the bond—you the lender. The issuer agrees to pay interest at a fixed rate, or *coupon rate*, at specified times, usually twice a year.

When the bond matures, the issuer must pay you the bond's face value—that is, the value that's marked on the bond—although you can sell the bond before it matures.

Most bonds mature in anywhere from one to 30 years. So-called notes are types of bonds that mature in 10 years or less.

You'll often hear the terms par value and current yield when dealing with bonds. Par value is the face value of a bond; current yield is the annual return a bond pays and is calculated as a percentage. To figure the yield, divide the income a bond pays in a year by the bond's current price.

Here are some more terms you should understand when it comes to bonds. Yield to maturity is the compound rate of return you'd have to earn on a comparable investment to equal the total return you'll get on your bond if you hold it until it matures. This yield takes into account the interest payments you receive as well as the net rise or fall in the price of the bond as it nears its maturity value.

As you might expect, the lower the quality rating of the bond and the longer the term to maturity the higher the interest rate.

Bonds are rated by two agencies: Standard & Poor's, which rates bonds from AAA to D, and Moody's Investor Services, which rates them from Aaa to D.

The higher the rating, the safer the bond, which means that the issuer is more likely to make the required annual interest payments and repay the principal when it comes due.

Safety, of course, carries a price—in this case, lower interest rates. Usually, the lower the rating, the higher the interest you'll earn. That's because companies with low-rated bonds must pay a high return to attract investors.

Sometimes, you can invest in a bond with a high rating and see its rating fall. This drop usually won't matter as long as you hold the bond until it matures. But if you decide to sell your bond before maturity, its principal value will fluctuate with the change in its rating.

Here's an example. Say you buy a bond with a Moody's Investor Services rating of A. Six months later, Moody's upgrades your bond's rating to Aa.

The bond is now considered a less risky investment than when you bought it, so the company that issued it may offer a lower yield on new bonds it offers.

That's good news for you if you want to sell. A buyer should be glad to pay more for your bond than you did, since the bond is now considered safer.

%

Now, say the rating on your bond fell.

In this case, the bond's value would fall as well. If you wanted to sell it before maturity, you would probably receive less than your purchase price. The buyer would have a bond with more risk; but, to compensate, it would pay a higher current yield.

As we saw, the value of a bond fluctuates with interest rates. Say, for example, that interest rates have shot up since you bought your bond.

To keep up with market rates, bond issuers must pay higher rates on new issues. So if you sell your bond before it matures, you'll get less than you paid for it.

Suppose you bought a $5,000 bond that pays 8 percent. A year later, market interest rates climb to 9 percent. Your bond, of course, continues to pay its coupon rate of 8 percent a year, or $400. But since investors can now buy bonds that pay 9 percent, the price of your bond drops.

You've probably heard bonds referred to as short-term, medium-term, and long-term. What do these terms mean? Usually short-term bonds mature in one to two years, medium-term bonds in two to seven years, and long-term bonds in more than 7 years.

You should know that, as a rule, a bond's value is affected by its maturity date. The price of long-term bonds—those that don't mature for many years—is influenced more by interest rate fluctuations than is the price of shorter-term bonds, as the following chart shows:

Underlying Value of Bond

Years to maturity	Market rate moves to 6%	Coupon rate is 8%	Market rate moves to 10%
1	$1,019	$1,000	$981
5	1,085	1,000	923
10	1,149	1,000	875
20	1,231	1,000	828
30	1,277	1,000	810

The chart makes the assumption that bonds of various maturities are worth $1,000 when they come due. It assumes, too, that you buy the bond when interest rates are 8 percent. The chart then shows what would happen to these bonds if interest rates fell to 6 percent or rose to 10 percent.

Since, as you can see, long-term bonds can be especially volatile, it usually makes sense to buy these bonds only if you plan to hold them to maturity to fund a specific long-term income need or goal.

If you *are* planning to hold your bonds until they mature, consider staggering their maturities, so they come

due at different times. That way, you won't be taking as much a chance on interest rates.

Say you want to allocate $100,000 of your portfolio to bonds. To stagger your maturities, you might take 35 percent of your $100,000, or $35,000, and buy five intermediate bonds—that is, bonds maturing in three to seven years. So you would purchase five $7,000 bonds that are slated to mature in three, four, five, six, and seven years.

Sixty-five percent of your $100,000 you would allocate to long-term bonds—those maturing in more than seven years. So you might buy three separate $20,000 bonds, maturing in 10, 12, and 15 years.

As we saw, long-term bonds are riskier than short-term ones, since, the longer the period of time, the harder it is to predict economic conditions. So bonds that have longer maturities usually offer a higher current yield than medium- or short-term bonds in order to attract buyers.

Finally, it's important to know what the terms "call provision" and "real rate of return" mean. If a bond has a call provision, the bond issuer can redeem it or call it before it matures. And that can be bad news for investors. Here's how.

Issuers usually call bonds when interest rates fall. That's because they can refinance their debt at the lower rate. But if your bond—with a high interest rate—is called, you must find another investment when interest rates are low.

Real rate of return is a bond's current yield less the current inflation rate and any taxes you pay on the interest your bond pays. In other words, real rate of return is the most accurate way to judge what your bond is actually paying you.

Since individual bonds are risky, you might want to protect yourself by diversifying; that is, you may want to put your retirement dollars in a bond mutual fund. Doing so makes sense particularly if you have less than $50,000 to invest.

Now that we have the basics out of the way, let's take a look at the types of bonds available for your retirement dollars.

What do you need to know about Treasury securities?

Securities issued by the U.S. government are the safest investment you can buy. If the United States defaults on its obligations, none of our investments would be worth anything. In other words, a government default is nearly impossible.

What's the difference between Treasury bills, notes,

and bonds. Bills mature in one year or less; notes in one to ten years; and Treasury bonds in ten to 30 years.

You may purchase Treasury notes and bonds directly from the Federal Reserve. Just call the Federal Reserve in the city nearest you to get information on the government's Treasury direct program. You can also write the Bureau of Public Debt, Department F, Washington, DC 20239-1200 to get a free brochure on this program.

You may find it more convenient to buy these securities from a bank or broker. If you do, however, you'll pay a small fee.

You'll pay federal taxes on income from Treasury securities, but the amount you receive is exempt from state and local taxes.

Among the advantages of these Treasury obligations: liquidity, safety, and a steady stream of income. Treasury obligations have other pluses as well. They're universally accepted as collateral for loans, for example.

The disadvantages? The biggest, perhaps, is that in exchange for rock-solid safety, you're accepting a yield that is about 0.75 to 1.50 percentage points lower than that of many corporate bonds.

Also, notes that mature in fewer than four years cost a minimum of $5,000. However, if you opt for longer maturities, you can buy these securities for only $1,000.

What do you need to know about municipal bonds?

Municipal bonds have long been the mainstay of people saving for retirement and those already in retirement. What could be better than bonds whose interest is free from federal income taxes and sometimes state and local taxes as well.

Today, however, there's one issue to consider when you think about buying municipal bonds. Uncle Sam now requires that part of your Social Security benefits be included in your taxable income if your adjusted gross income, plus 50 percent of your benefits and any tax-exempt interest, tops a certain level. So a tax-exempt investment may not always pay off if you're collecting Social Security.

Apart from this consideration, are tax-exempt bonds a good deal for you if you're in a high marginal bracket? Usually, they are, but you must run the numbers to know for sure.

To compare the yields of taxable and tax-exempt bonds, you convert the yield on the tax-free bonds to an equivalent taxable yield. Doing so is simple. You just divide the tax-exempt yield by 1 minus your tax bracket (expressed as a decimal).

Here's an example. Say you're in the 28 percent tax

bracket, and you're considering purchasing a tax-exempt bond with a 6 percent yield.

You divide 6 percent by 1 minus your tax bracket (28 percent)—or 0.72. The result—8.33—is the amount you must get from a taxable bond to match the interest from a municipal bond. So if you can find a taxable bond that pays more than 8.33 percent, go for it. If not, it probably makes more sense to buy the tax-exempt bond.

Here's something else you should know. Public-purpose municipal bonds are also exempt from state and local taxes if they're issued by your home state. The only exceptions to this rule are Illinois, Iowa, Kansas, Nebraska, Oklahoma, Pennsylvania and Wisconsin.

Moreover, if you live in Alaska, Florida, Indiana, Kentucky, Nevada, New Hampshire, New Mexico, North Dakota, Pennsylvania, South Dakota, Texas, Utah, Washington, or Wyoming, out-of-state public-purpose bonds are also exempt from state taxes.

Municipal bonds that are free from both federal and state taxes are advertised as double-tax free. Those that are exempt from federal, state, and local taxes are, appropriately enough, known as triple tax-free.

Most public-purpose municipal bonds are reasonably free of risk and liquid but you pay steep commissions when you sell. Some, however, are riskier than others.

So-called general obligation bonds are the least risky,

since they're backed by the full faith and credit of the government that issues them. Revenue bonds, however, are backed only by the income from the project they're set up to finance—a local hospital, for example, or a water or sewer project. If the project fails, you could lose the entire amount you invested.

What about insured municipal bonds? You don't pay for the insurance—the issuer does. However, for your added measure of safety, you must be prepared to accept a yield one-tenth to one-third of a percentage point less than on uninsured bonds.

Municipal bonds aren't cheap. They sell in units of $5,000, but you can get around this hurdle by investing in mutual funds that invest in municipal bonds. You can find funds that allow you to invest as little as $500 to $1,000.

What do you need to know about corporate bonds?

A corporate bond, as one might expect, is a bond issued by a corporation. The purchaser of the bond is, in effect, lending money to the corporation in exchange for its promise to repay the purchaser that amount plus interest at some future date.

%

When you buy a corporate bond, you're usually purchasing one of two varieties—a so-called debenture or what's known as a mortgage bond.

Debentures are backed only by the integrity of the corporation. A mortgage bond, by contrast, is secured by a mortgage on the corporation's assets.

Corporate bonds are riskier than bonds issued by the U.S. government. If the company issuing your bond goes belly up, you may get your money back—or you may not.

It depends on the provisions of the bond you buy. Bondholders do usually take priority over common stockholders when a company's assets are distributed. However, in practice, few people below the level of creditor receive any compensation when a company goes bankrupt.

As you might expect, to compensate for this extra risk, corporate bonds pay higher yields than government bonds. And, as with other types of bonds, the lower the bonds are rated by Standard and Poor's or Moody's, the higher the yield.

Most corporations issue bonds in denominations of $1,000, but you must buy them in lots of five. And you pay taxes on the income you receive at your ordinary rate.

Corporate bonds are liquid. You can usually sell them

without too much trouble before they mature. Bonds that carry the highest ratings are the most liquid.

What do you need to know about high-yield bonds?

A high-yield bond is a special type of corporate bonds, known familiarly as a "junk bond." These instruments pay very high yields, and for good reason. They're usually rated anywhere from BBB or Baa or lower by Standard & Poor's or Moody's.

As you can guess, the risk you take on when you purchase these bonds is very high. If the company goes bust, you'll probably lose every penny you invested. What if the company defaults on its bonds? You probably won't receive the interest promised to you but your principal may remain intact.

Within the past year, defaults on these low-grade corporate bonds were much higher than defaults on other corporate bonds. And, with the collapse of the investment bank of Drexel Burnham Lambert in 1989, the outlook for these bonds have become even more uncertain.

That's because the firm maintained a market for these bonds. When it fell, the market became chaotic. While yields are still high, the value of many of these bonds has plunged.

%

What do you need to know about convertible bonds?

Convertible bonds give you the best of both worlds. They're part bond and part stock, and, because of their hybrid nature, you can buy them for current income, but have the chance to pocket a profit later if the issuer's stock appreciates. Here's how these bonds work.

When you own a convertible bond, the company issuing it grants you the right to exchange your bonds for shares of the company's common stock. The tradeoff for this privilege; a lower yield.

You can make the exchange when, and if, the stock's price rises a certain amount above the stock's price when the bond was first issued.

What do you need to know about zero-coupon bonds?

These bonds are an excellent investment for part of your retirement portfolio, as long as you don't need interest income currently to support your lifestyle.

What are these bonds? Zero-coupon bonds are simply bonds without a coupon rate. When you buy them, you receive no periodic annual interest.

Instead, the bonds are sold at a deep discount from face value, much like U.S. savings bonds. For example, you might pay $275 for a $1,000 bond that yields 9 percent and matures in 15 years. When the bond matures, you know exactly the amount you'll collect. That's one reason these bonds make sense in tax-deferred retirement accounts.

Here's another reason that you may find more compelling. The law says that you must pay taxes on the interest you would collect each year on zero-coupon bonds, even though you don't actually receive any money until the bond matures. The only exception to this rule: zeros issued by a municipality, since that interest is tax-exempt.

However, if you buy these bonds for a tax-sheltered retirement account, such as an IRA or Keogh, you don't have to worry about paying annual taxes.

Zero-coupon securities come in nearly as many varieties as there are bonds. So you can buy corporate zeros, municipal zeros, convertible zeros, mortgage-backed zeros, and Treasury zeros. If you're interested in buying the safest bonds possible, stick to Treasury zeros.

If you hold your zero coupon bond to maturity, you don't have to worry about fluctuations in interest rates. You'll collect the amount you're due when the bond matures.

However, if you plan to sell before maturity, watch out. The value of zero-coupon bonds fluctuates much more dramatically than other bonds. So if rates rise, you could lose big if you had to sell your bond before it matures. If they fall? You could make a killing.

Here's the reason. Because the bonds are locked in at a specific—and favorable—reinvestment rate, investors are willing to pay more for them than for other bonds in periods of falling interest rates.

When you buy zero-coupon bonds, expect to pay a sales commission. Make sure you ask your broker what the fee is, since it's often included in the price of the bond.

What do you need to know about mortgage-backed securities?

These securities are a type of government bond, but, as we'll see, they carry varying degrees of risks.

Mortgage-backed securities are pools of home mortgages.

Here's how they work.

The Government National Mortgage Association (GNMA or Ginnie Mae), Federal National Mortgage Association (FNMA or Fannie Mae), and the Federal Home Loan Mortgage Corporation (FHLMC or Freddie Mac) all buy mortgages from banks and thrifts, pool them, then sell units of the pools to investors. They're all a little different, so let's run through the three types of securities.

When you buy Ginnie Maes, you're actually purchasing a portion of the 30-year mortgages insured by the U.S. Federal Housing Administration (FHA) and the Veterans Administration (VA).

The Government National Mortgage Association collects monthly interest and principal payments that homeowners pay on their property, subtracts a small administrative fee, and passes the payments on to its investors.

Since homeowners' monthly payments include both principal and interest, the check investors receive each month includes both interest income and some principal.

The amount of principal and interest a Ginnie Mae pays each month fluctuates, since some homeowners always pay off their mortgages because they sell or refinance their houses.

So if you invest in Ginnie Maes, you can't predict precisely how much you'll receive each month. But Uncle Sam is understanding. To compensate you for this uncertainty, Ginnie Maes pay more than U.S. Treasury bonds.

And they're just as safe as Treasury bonds, because, they're backed by the full faith and credit of the United States government.

%

Ginnie Maes can be a sensible way to get higher yields without sacrificing safety. But their cost—$25,000—puts them out of reach for many small investors. That's why many people invest in Ginnie Mae mutual funds or unit investment trusts (UIT) that buy Ginnie Maes. You can invest in one of these funds for as little as $500 to $1,000.

Fannie Maes and Freddie Macs are so-called mortgage-backed securities. Unlike Ginnie Mae's, which return both interest and principal each month, these securities pay regular interest payments. But, like most bonds, you don't receive your principal back until the securities mature.

Fannie Maes and Freddie Macs invest in mortgages that aren't insured by the Federal Housing Administration or the Veterans Administration. That means they carry more risk than Ginnie Maes. Even though the mortgage isn't guaranteed, however, the Federal National Mortgage Association (Fannie Mae) and the Federal Home Loan Mortgage Corporation (Freddie Mac) do guarantee that you'll receive your interest payments. Because these securities are more risky, they pay about one-half of a percentage point more in interest than does a Ginnie Mae.

Fannie Maes and Freddie Macs, like Ginnie Maes, also cost $25,000 each. But, again like Ginnie Maes, you can invest in mutual funds that purchase Fannie Maes and Freddie Macs for a small initial amount—typically $500 to $1,000.

There's one other type of security you should know about. This security is issued by state housing agencies in order to raise money for low-interest loans for low-income and first-time homebuyers. The big advantage of these bonds? They're exempt from federal taxes and exempt from state taxes in the issuing state.

So, you ask, what's the bottom line?

Mortgage-backed securities pay a better yield than other government securities, and you don't give up much in safety. Not only are these securities backed by the government, they're also collateralized by the real estate they finance.

Ginnie Maes, Fannie Maes and Freddie Macs are also liquid. You shouldn't have much trouble selling them should the need arise. Of course, like any other bond, you can lose some of your principal if you sell before maturity when interest rates have climbed.

What do you need to know about annuities?

An annuity is a contract underwritten by an insurance company.

Although annuities come in a variety of types, the two

primary ones are immediate annuities and deferred annuities. With an immediate annuity, you usually purchase the contract with a lump sum and begin receiving benefits 30 to 90 days later.

A deferred annuity, on the other hand, pays you benefits starting at some future date, usually at retirement.

You buy your annuity contract by paying a lump sum, making installment payments, or through some combination of the two.

With a fixed annuity, the amount you receive is paid out in regular equal installments. You decide how frequently you want to receive payments. For example, you may decide to collect payments monthly or quarterly. Or you may opt for annual payments.

Annuity payments are made to you either over a fixed period—20 years, say—or over an indefinite period, such as the remainder of your life.

The terms are spelled out in your annuity contract.

Annuities are available from a variety of sources—insurance companies, banks, and brokerage firms.

With an annuity, the interest, dividends, and capital gains you earn accumulate tax-deferred until they're paid to you under the terms of your annuity.

Your annuity is as safe as the insurance company underwriting it. So check the fiscal health of the company before you plunk down your hard-earned dollars.

Let's look in the next chapter at our third category of investment: equities.

16

The Equity Portion of Your Portfolio

Maybe you've heard people say that you shouldn't invest in equities at all after you retire. That's another one of those old realities that doesn't hold true today.

Why not?

The reason is we're living longer, which means we're spending more time in retirement. So we need to keep some of our money invested in equities, because that's one of the best ways to beat inflation over the long haul. What about risk? As we will see later in this chapter, your risk decreases as your time horizon for investing increases.

You'll probably want to divide the portion of your portfolio allocated to equities, the third major category of investments, across different categories of stock—income stocks, growth stocks, growth and income stocks, and aggressive growth stocks.

Let's take a look at these different categories.

What are income stocks?

These stocks produce steady income in the form of dividends. As a rule, these are the stocks of older, well-established companies in mature industries such as utilities and railroads. Because they don't need cash to support rapid expansion, these companies tend to return a hefty portion of their earnings to investors in the form of quarterly cash dividends. Income stocks are usually less risky—at least in the short run—than the stocks of younger, less well-established companies.

The downside? As you might expect, they offer little chance for growth. In other words, don't expect the price of your stock to appreciate too much.

The reason they don't grow very fast is that demand for the products or services of these companies is fairly stable. That's why income stocks often form the backbone of the conservative investor's portfolio.

What are growth-and-income stocks?

As their name suggests, these stocks combine regular dividend payments with some prospect for growth. They're slightly riskier than income stocks only in that the market value of their shares is subject to greater variation.

You've no doubt heard the term, blue-chip *stocks*, which are also known as widow-and-orphan stocks. These are the equities most people think of when they refer to growth-and-income stocks.

Don't ask your broker for a list of blue-chip stocks, though. It doesn't exist. But companies whose stock might qualify for that designation are American Telephone & Telegraph, Coca-Cola, Dow Chemical, Du Pont, General Electric, General Mills, ITT, and Merck.

All these companies have a proven track record of stable growth, steady profits, and regular dividend payments.

What are growth stocks?

When companies are young and growing quickly, they rarely pay dividends. They need the cash to finance their own growth.

But if their growth strategies are successful, the value of their stock can increase substantially—and quickly.

These are the companies you'll find on such lists as the annual Inc. 100 or the *Forbes* list of up-and-comers.

But what moves up quickly can also move down quickly. Growth companies are taking risks, which means that some of them will stumble. Their stock prices can be volatile, so you should be prepared for values to dip and soar.

Growth stocks usually have higher Price/earnings (P/E) ratios than other equities, which means that a dollar of earnings for a growth stock results in a higher stock price than for a growth-and-income stock. Growth stocks make few or no dividend payments to shareholders. That means you shouldn't rely on growth stocks for current income, but they can be a valuable part of a portfolio that's oriented toward long-term growth.

What are aggressive growth stocks?

Everything we said about growth stocks above applies in spades to aggressive growth stocks. These are issued by very young companies, often operating on the cutting edge of technology, where the risks of failure are as great as the potential rewards of success.

Yes

I want to learn more about Price Waterhouse's personal financial management programs. Please send me more information about:

☐ **Personal Financial Analysis**

A comprehensive financial plan (for people still working) which addresses tax strategies, investments, retirement, life and disability insurance, estate planning, and education funding.

☐ **Retirement Planning Analysis**

A highly-focused financial plan (for people still working) which determines the savings and investment strategies necessary to achieve *your* retirement goals.

NAME

ADDRESS

CITY STATE ZIP

DAYTIME PHONE

OPTIONAL INFORMATION:

AGE: _____ SEX: ☐ M ☐ F I AM: ☐ EMPLOYED ☐ SELF-EMPLOYED

HOUSEHOLD INCOME: ☐ LESS THAN $40,000 ☐ $40,000 - $79,999 ☐ $80,000 - $120,000 ☐ OVER $120,000

NO POSTAGE
NECESSARY
IF MAILED
IN THE
UNITED STATES

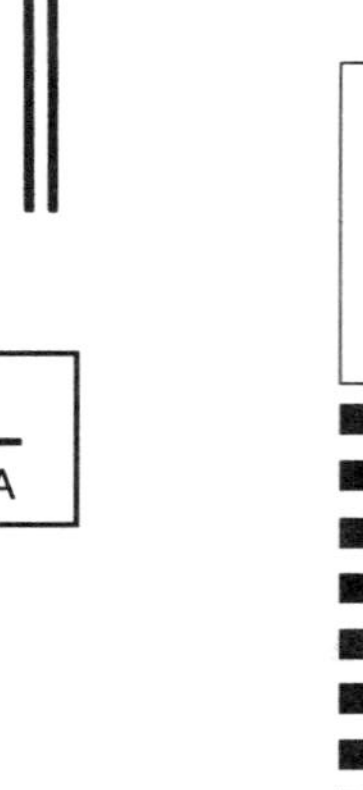

BUSINESS REPLY MAIL

FIRST CLASS MAIL PERMIT NO 43037 WALTHAM MA

POSTAGE WILL BE PAID BY ADDRESSEE

Price Waterhouse
University Office Park
51 Sawyer Road
P O Box 9095
Waltham MA 02254-9870

What is the New York Stock Exchange?

The New York Stock Exchange, or NYSE, is the oldest of the stock exchanges. Stocks that trade on the Big Board, as it's known, usually belong to older, established companies—a General Electric, say, or Motorola.

Dow Jones, publisher of the Wall Street Journal, includes 30 NYSE stocks in its oft-quoted industrial average. Here's the list, arranged alphabetically: Alcoa, Allied-Signal, AT&T, American Express, Bethlehem Steel, Boeing, Chevron, Coca-Cola, DuPont, Exxon, General Electric, and General Motors.

Also, Goodyear, IBM, International Paper, Kodak, McDonald's, Merck, Minnesota Mining, Navistar, Philip Morris, Primerica, Procter & Gamble, Sears Robuck, Texaco, Union Carbide, United Technology, USX Corp., Westinghouse, and Woolworth. This list represents 15-20% of NYSE stocks and are stocks that Dow Jones believes are indicative of the market as a whole.

What is the American Stock Exchange?

Stocks that trade on the American Stock Exchange or AMEX must have a market price of at least $5 and companies listed on this exchange must have a net worth of at least $4 million and earnings of at least $400,000.

Usually, shares of established small- and medium-sized companies trade on the AMEX.

What is the over-the-counter market?

The over-the-counter market is nothing more than a nationwide network of brokers and dealers who buy and sell stocks that usually aren't sold on either the NYSE or the AMEX. The National Association of Securities Dealers (NASD) regulates this market.

NASDAQ, the National Association of Securities Dealers Automated Quotations System, is a computerized network that's owned by the NASD and provides stockbrokers and dealers with price quotations for over-the-counter securities.

How risky are equities?

The answer depends on how long you invest. Take a look at the chart below. It illustrates how you risk declines the longer you invest.

MARKET RISK
COMMON STOCKS—TIME HORIZONS
1926–1988

Length	*Total*	*Holding Periods Winners*	*Losers*
1 Year	63	42	21
5 Years	59	45	14
10 Years	54	47	7
20 Years	44	44	0

Based on The S & P 500

Source: Ibbotson Associates, SBBI 1989 Yearbook

Now, on to our next category of investments—hard assets.

17

Hard Assets

As the term implies, hard assets are those that you can see and touch: gold, silver, and other precious metals; oil and gas; real estate; and collectibles. Once you decide you should allocate a portion of your assets to hard assets, you need to figure out which you want to purchase.

Most people buy the type of hard asset with which they're familiar. If they're used to investing in real estate, for instance, they'll continue to buy real estate. In this chapter, we tell you what you need to know about the various types of hard assets.

Oil and gas

There are three ways you can invest in oil and gas, short of drilling for oil and gas yourself: through stock in energy companies, a stake in limited partnerships, or shares in master limited partnerships.

A simple way to participate in the oil and gas industry is to buy energy stocks, which make up about 18 percent of the Standard & Poor's 500 composite stock index. A major advantage of this strategy is liquidity. You can buy and sell any amount whenever you want.

The downside? Energy stocks may not directly reflect changes in oil and gas prices. And they're subject to the vagaries of the stock market as a whole.

You can participate more directly in this industry through oil and gas "programs" or drilling partnerships. These programs share some characteristics with mutual funds.

Both are investment pools run by professional managers. Both pass through profits and losses to investors, and both have diversified holdings.

But that's where the similarities end.

The purpose of oil and gas programs is generally either to explore or drill for oil or purchase producing oil wells. Usually these programs come in the form of joint ventures or "untraded" limited partnerships. That is, they're offered for a fixed number of months. Then, after closing, they're no longer traded on public exchanges.

So each program is a distinct operating business, varying in size from $1 million up to $300 million. Partnership units usually cost a minimum of $5,000 to $10,000.

Who offers these programs? They're put together and offered to investors either by independent oil companies or by oil investment managers.

Gold

What are the advantages of investing in precious gold? Since it has intrinsic value, it's a hedge against inflation and political uncertainties. Also, gold is a liquid investment. There's an active market for gold, so you can sell it any time you want.

You can invest in gold in a number of ways.

You can purchase bullion—gold bars or ingots—or coins directly. Or you can buy certificates from a dealer who holds on to the gold for you. You can purchase gold futures. You can buy gold mining stocks—or invest in mutual funds that invest in gold mining stocks.

When you buy gold bullion, you buy gold outright. You can hold it in a depository in the United States or in a foreign banking center, such as London or Zurich.

Buying gold coins is far more practical. Among your choices: the Canadian maple leaf, the U.S. gold eagle, the Mexican peso, and the Chinese panda. All these coins are sold for a premium above the value of their gold content.

Of course, if you buy gold directly, you get no current return—an important consideration for people who are already retired. Shares in gold mining companies can be another story. They frequently pay dividends—some of them quite generous.

Precious metals

Most people who invest in metals put their money in gold. But you can also invest in silver and platinum—and in much the same way. Again, your options are bullion, coins, certificates, metals futures, mining stocks, and mutual funds that invest in mining stocks.

Real estate

Let's face it. Not everyone is cut out to be a landlord. Many people have neither the time nor the temperament to cope with dripping faucets and broken windows.

And making money buying and selling properties isn't the sure thing it was in many locations just a few years ago. In most parts of the country, even in formerly

"hot" markets, prices are beginning to level off or head downward.

Having said that, we should also point out that buying and selling property directly can still yield rewards for investors if you're in the right place at the right time. Just be aware that direct ownership also entails the biggest risks.

For instance, you buy a small apartment building. You figure the rents you collect will pay off your mortgage. A few years down the road, you'll sell the building at a profit. How can you lose? Easily.

For one, a number of factors—an increase in supply over demand, say—may suddenly cause rents in your area to plummet. But you must still pay your mortgage. And that cash will have to come out of your own pocket.

Because real estate is such a risky and time-consuming proposition, it's a good idea not to go into it alone. In fact, only if you have plenty of cash to spend on repairs and ample time to devote to details, such as broken windows, should you try direct ownership.

And you should go in with realistic expectations. Many people who buy rental apartments or houses lose money. They find their rental income just isn't enough to cover mortgage payments and other costs such as capital improvements and other repairs, so they need the added plus of tax breaks just to come out even. And the tax breaks for rental property are a lot less favorable today than they were a few years ago.

How do you figure out if a real-estate deal is a good one? And what should you look for in valuing property? Here are some ideas.

Never—and we mean never—buy real estate without studying the market where you plan to buy. Ideally, you should live in an area for several years or research it thoroughly before you even consider purchasing property there. A firm grasp of local conditions can prevent you from making costly mistakes.

And, of course, have the property inspected by experts for structural, termite, or any other damage before you buy. You also need to know how well the current owners maintained the property. Are the heating and cooling systems and kitchen appliances all in good working order?

The fact is, if you're in for major repairs, you need to know before you plunk your money down. Also, if major repairs are needed, you may negotiate a lower purchase price. Inspectors charge no more than $100 to $200. And it is money well spent.

Real-estate investment trusts

If you don't want to invest in real estate directly, you may want to consider real-estate investment trusts, or REITs.

Real-estate investment trusts combine the best features of the Wall Street stock markets with Main Street's realty markets. They're liquid investments traded daily on the stock exchanges. But they also offer all the benefits of otherwise illiquid income-producing real estate.

Here's how they work. Investing in a REIT is similar to investing in a mutual fund. You pool your money with that of other investors to buy and/or finance income-producing properties, such as office buildings and apartments.

Rental income from these properties goes to the REIT to pay its expenses. The remainder goes to you in the form of dividends.

And so does the interest the REIT may receive from any mortgages it writes. (Some REITs, known as mortgage REITs, take investors' funds and write mortgages. In effect, they act as bankers, charging interest to owners for use of the funds and distributing the net income to you.)

Gains from the sale of properties are also passed along to you as dividends. As dividends increase, so usually does the price of your REIT shares, but you should know that shares could fluctuate due to interest rate changes and other factors.

Through the combination of generous dividends and price appreciation, REITs can reward investors with an average current return of 6 to 8 percent annually, usually partially tax-sheltered. But beware: As you might expect, REITs aren't always this successful.

One large REIT, for instance, invested heavily in real estate in oil-producing states. When real-estate prices there plummeted, the REIT collapsed. The result: Investors may have lost every penny. Again, what matters in real-estate investments are the underlying properties.

Most REIT shares are easy to buy and sell. You do it the same way you buy and sell shares of corporate stock—through a broker.

The biggest advantages of many REITs over other forms of real-estate investing are liquidity and a lack of headaches. Investors in REITs avoid late-night telephone calls from disgruntled tenants. Also, you may sell your shares at any time, but the price you receive may vary considerably with the market value of underlying assets. So REITs are, for the most part, a very liquid way of investing in a traditionally illiquid asset. And, REITs usually allow you to spread your risk by buying into a diverse portfolio of properties.

So if you have limited assets, need liquidity, and

think real estate is a sound investment, REITs may be for you. But there are drawbacks to the trusts. Primary among them: The value of REIT shares—like stocks—fluctuates with expectations for earnings and with equity market as a whole.

Also, earnings from REITs may fall below those of limited partnerships, which we'll discuss next. One reason is partnerships may buy and sell properties at will, but REITs may have to hold some of their properties for four years.

Real-estate syndications

Real-estate syndications, like real-estate investment trusts, may invest in a host of properties—hotels, motels, office buildings, nursing homes, and so on.

What are their advantages?

They offer most of the benefits of owning real estate, including tax breaks, but you escape the burden of managing the property and the personal liabilities of an owner.

Still, real-estate syndications are limited partnerships. And when you invest in a limited partnership, you often turn your dollars over to someone else to manage for five or more years.

What if you want out early? Traditionally, you had to

get permission to sell from the general partner. And the market for limited partnership interests was thin. But in recent years, a secondary market for some partnerships has developed. So getting out may be easier, but you still recoup only 40 percent to 60 percent of your investment.

Partnerships generally are riskier than REITs, because of the lack of liquidity and lack of diversification. Partnerships also require a hefty minimum investment, typically $5,000 and up, compared to a per share price of less than $100 for many REITs.

Should you choose a REIT over an income-oriented syndication? There's something to be said for both investments.

Some REITs carry low management fees (the fees are included in the syndication or REIT per-share price). And, of course, REITs are generally liquid.

The advantages of syndications: Their return is based on the underlying value of the property. So they generally aren't affected by the vagaries of the stock market. And they can shelter some cash flow or pass along any tax losses to investors.

If you want to test the waters—and can afford it—you should carefully study the syndicator's track record. The offering prospectus will contain this information.

We've discussed so far how to invest directly in our

four asset allocation categories. But there's an easy way to have a professional manage your investments *and* provide you with instant diversification as well. In the next chapter, we'll give you the lowdown on mutual funds.

18

What You Need to Know About Mutual Funds

An increasingly popular option for people looking for a place to put the dollars they're investing for retirement is mutual funds.

Mutual funds provide an easy way to invest in the different asset categories—cash, fixed-income, equities, and hard assets—or some combination of categories.

Mutual funds today come in a host of varieties and cover a broad range of investment types. You can find what you need if you're twenty-five and retirement seems light-years away—or seventy-five and eager to preserve your current income.

Why invest in mutual funds?

They offer many advantages. You get expert management of your money, for one. Your money is handled by people who devote their full time and attention to the task.

You also get diversification. To offset the business risk associated with individual equities, you'd have to purchase a minimum of 15 separate stocks. With a mutual fund, you get instant diversification. Here's why. The rules allow mutual funds to purchase no more than 5% of the shares of any single company. The rules also say that a mutual fund can invest no more than 5% of its assets in any one company.

And you get convenience. Putting money in and taking money out of a mutual fund is almost as easy as depositing money in and withdrawing money from your corner bank or savings and loan.

What is a mutual fund?

Many investors include both *open-end* and *closed-end mutual funds* in their definition of mutual funds, although, technically, the two are different legal entities. Both, however, accumulate pools of money from investors and invest these dollars in a wide range of vehicles, such as stocks, bonds and money-market securities.

Open-end mutual funds sell an unlimited number of new shares and constantly repurchase or redeem outstanding ones. So the amount of money under their management is always changing.

With closed-end companies, the amount of money under management is relatively fixed. These companies raise money as ordinary corporations do—through public offerings.

Also, once they're issued, the shares of closed-end companies are traded just like any other stocks—on the New York and American stock exchanges and over the counter.

Closed-end companies and open-end mutual funds share one important characteristic: They can both be classified by their investment objectives.

How are shares priced?

If you look at your newspaper's listing of mutual funds, you'll see listed under the price the letters NAV, which stand for net asset value per share.

Net asset value per share is calculated by subtracting a fund's total liabilities from its total assets, then dividing the result by the number of shares outstanding.

Open-end funds usually sell or redeem their shares at

NAV, less any applicable deferred sales charges or redemption fees.

But closed-end funds sell for an amount that's higher (that is, they carry a premium) or lower (they sell at a discount) than their NAV. It all depends on what the market thinks of the fund. Historically, most closed-end funds have sold at a discount.

In other words, the price of closed-end funds—like the stock price of other companies—is determined by supply and demand. Closed-end funds do not redeem their shares upon request.

☞ CAUTION You should keep in mind that if you invest in either a closed-end or open-end mutual fund, it isn't the same as investing in, say, a certificate of deposit. With a CD, the face value of your principal won't fluctuate. With a mutual fund, there are no such guarantees, although money-market funds traditionally have maintained a constant NAV.

How do you evaluate funds?

Your primary criteria for selecting a mutual fund should be its historical total return and the risk associated with that return.

So you should compare funds' three-year-, five-year-, and ten-year return. You want to see how the fund you're considering has performed in both bull and bear markets.

When you evaluate the risk associated with the historical return, you're really looking at the fund's volatility.

Say you're interested in two funds, both of the same type (aggressive growth, say), and both have the same average annual total return for the past 10 years. Which should you select? Pick the fund that's least volatile. In other words, a fund that turns in a consistent 10 percent a year is preferable to one that earns 15 percent one year and 5 percent the next.

What other factors should you consider when investing in mutual funds?

Return and risk matter most when it comes to selecting a fund. But you may want to be aware of some other factors, such as the fund's turnover rate, meaning the average length of time the fund holds shares before selling them. A high turnover rate sometimes indicates that the fund manager is trying to time the market—that is, judge when the market is going to go up or down—and market timing just doesn't work consistently.

You may also want to consider investing in a fund that

is part of a family, especially where one is a money-market fund.

What is a fund family? A mutual-fund family is simply a group of two or more mutual funds offered through the same sponsor organization. In most cases, the goals of the funds differ. For example, one may be a growth fund, the other an income fund.

With a family, you can easily move your money from one investment vehicle to another—sometimes with no more than a telephone call.

You should also check to see if a fund or fund family offers free 800 numbers.

Two other criteria to keep in mind: the performance history of the fund manager—the longer he or she has been at the helm, the better—and the age of the fund. You should always approach newer funds with no track record with caution.

You can also subscribe to a number of ranking services that evaluate mutual fund performances. Among them: *CDA Mutual Fund Report* (monthly), 11501 Georgia Ave., Silver Spring, MD 20902 (301) 975-9600 and *Mutual Fund Values* (biweekly), 53 W. Jackson Blvd, Chicago, IL 60604 (312) 427-1985. And several magazines, including *Forbes, Money*, and *Business Week* provide extensive annual rankings of mutual funds.

What fees do you pay?

Obviously, mutual-fund managers don't provide their services for free. The cost of operating a mutual fund is passed along to investors. In addition, some funds impose sales charges and redemption fees.

Since funds have different charges for buying, holding, and redeeming shares, it makes sense to find out about a fund's fee structure before you invest.

The best sources of information on charges are the fund's prospectus and a supplementary document known as the "Statement of Additional Information." Ask for a copy of both, as well as the latest annual and interim reports to shareholders.

What are annual charges?

To help pay their operating expenses, mutual funds charge annual fees. These service charges generally add up to 0.5% for a bond fund and from 1% to 1.5 percent for an equity fund. You'll find annual fees described in the fund's prospectus as a percentage of net assets and, sometimes, on a per share basis.

What are front-end loads?

When you buy mutual-fund shares from a stockbroker or other salesperson, you usually pay a *front-end load*—that is, a commission on the shares you purchase. In addition, you frequently pay a sales charge even when you invest directly in funds offered by some financial services companies.

Here's an example of how a front-end load works. Say you instruct your stockbroker to invest $3,000 into a mutual fund whose shares have a net asset value of $50 each.

Your $3,000 will get you 60 shares, right? Wrong.

To purchase shares in some funds, you pay an initial sales charge, which is levied on the total amount you invest. Let's say the sales charge is the maximum allowable, 8.5 percent and adds up to $255. So only $2,745 of your money actually goes to purchase shares.

If you buy more shares in the same fund from a broker or salesperson, chances are you will pay a reduced sales commission. Why? Many funds offer discounts on sales charges, based on the total amount you have invested.

With low-load funds, expect to pay an initial sales charge of 0.5 percent to 3.0 percent. No-load funds levy no up front sales charges, but a few impose a redemption fee of up to 1.0 percent.

You should know that there's no evidence that load

funds perform any better or any worse than low-load or no-load funds.

What are back-end loads?

Some funds impose back-end loads or deferred sales charges when you take your money out. These fees vary widely but are usually based on how long you hold your shares. For example, if you pull out in the first year of your investment, you pay more than if you pull out after four years.

Funds that impose back-end loads typically charge 6 percent if you withdraw your money within one year. This percentage usually decreases 1 percent each year until it reaches zero after six years. Since back-end loads decrease over time, they usually are less than front-end loads if you stay in the fund for a longer period. Often they are combined with 12b-1 fees.

What are 12b-1 fees?

Many mutual funds charge an annual 12b-1 fee. This fee takes its prosaic name from the Securities and Exchange Commission rule that allows its use. It may be used by the fund sponsor to cover the cost of compensating salespeople and advertising the fund.

Now that you know how different investments work, let's take a look at how to construct an allocation to match your own circumstances. As you'll see, mutual funds enable you to allocate your assets within each investment category.

19

An Allocation to Match Your Profile

You've learned the basics of asset allocation, or diversification. And you understand the ins and outs of the four asset allocation categories.

Now, it's time to apply what you've learned to your own circumstances. Where do you begin? Start by taking these seven factors into account:

- Your goals and objectives, including those not related to your retirement, such as helping your children purchase their first home
- Your tolerance for risk
- Your pension expectations
- Your prospects for other income, such as from a part-time job

- The number of years you have until you retire
- The number of years you're likely to spend in retirement
- The amount of time you have to invest

Then adjust your allocation as these factors change.

Following are three sample asset allocation cases. Keep in mind that they are samples only but they illustrate how to construct an allocation, and evaluate the factors that go into it.

Remember that your allocation should shield you from the business risk associated with some investments. It should also preserve the purchasing power of your dollars during retirement, plus serve as a genuine hedge against inflation.

One more important point: Don't confuse asset allocations as we discuss them here with asset allocations proposed by some big Wall Street firms.

Those firms tout so-called "tactical" asset allocations—that is, allocations that aren't tailored to your individual circumstances and that involve an element of market timing. As you remember from Chapter 11, market timing doesn't work.

Still another important point: You should include all of your investable assets in your allocation, including

those in all of your retirement plans (such as IRAs, 401(k), profit sharing and so on).

CASE A

Mike and Susan are both 52 years old, and their goal is to retire when Mike turns 62 with an income of $56,000 a year. Mike doesn't have a company-provided pension, and Susan doesn't work outside the home.

They subtract their Social Security benefits—$15,000 a year—to get the amount they need from their investments each year after Mike retires—$41,000.

Next, they add up their investable assets—$75,000 in a 401(k) plan, $200,000 in a profit-sharing plan, $18,000 in stock options, and $120,000 in other investable assets. The total comes to $413,000. If those assets are to generate the $41,000 a year they need after retirement, they must grow substantially.

Now, say, their tolerance for risk is high, and their current asset allocation looks like this:

Cash and cash equivalents	25 percent
Fixed-income vehicles	5 percent
Equities	70 percent
Hard assets	0 percent

How should they change their allocation? For starters, they need a more balanced portfolio. Mike and Susan took a look at their allocation and here's how they changed it:

Cash and cash equivalents	10 percent
Fixed-income vehicles	30 percent
Equities	45 percent
Hard assets	15 percent

But Mike and Susan aren't finished yet. They now must decide how to allocate their assets within the equity and fixed income categories.

Since Mike and Susan are investing for a long period of time, and their tolerance for risk is high, they also put more of the dollars earmarked for equities in growth and aggressive growth stocks.

In the fixed-income category, most of their dollars are invested in intermediate-term vehicles but they do begin to allocate a small percentage to long-term bonds to begin to lock in a steady stream of income for their retirement. This amount can be added to as they get closer to retirement which is still over 10 years away.

CASE B

Jim and Karen are both 54 years old. She's self-employed; he works for a large corporation. Their goal is to retire at age 65 with an annual income of $72,000. Social Security will help—the two of them can count on a total of $23,000 a year from Uncle Sam—and so will Jim's company pension—$24,000 a year.

But, they still need $25,000 a year—that is, $72,000 minus Social Security benefits of $23,000 and a company pension of $24,000—to meet their retirement goal.

And this money must come from their investments. Their current assets add up to $345,000—$100,000 in a 401(k) plan, $15,000 in an ESOP, $80,000 in a Keogh, and $150,000 in other investable assets. Their tolerance for risk is low, so their current allocation looks like this:

Cash and cash equivalents	30 percent
Fixed-income vehicles	60 percent
Equities	10 percent
Hard assets	0

How should they change their allocation? They need to invest more dollars in equities and hard assets as a hedge against inflation.

Here's the allocation they came up with:

Cash and cash equivalents	15 percent
Fixed-income vehicles	40 percent
Equities	35 percent
Hard assets	10 percent

CASE C

Roger is 58 years old, divorced, and his goal is to retire—in two short years—at the age of 60 with an annual income of $36,000.

Of this amount, how much must he generate from his investments? Subtract Social Security benefits of $9,600 and a company pension of $20,000 from his retirement goal of $36,000. The answer—$6,400—is the amount of retirement income that must come from his investments.

Now, let's add up his investable assets—$75,000 in a 401(k), $25,000 in an IRA, and $100,000 in other investable assets—or a total of $200,000.

His current asset allocation looks like this:

Cash and cash equivalents	30 percent
Fixed-income vehicles	20 percent
Equities	30 percent
Hard assets	20 percent

How should he change his allocation? Since he'll need a steady stream of income when he retires in two short years, he shifts dollars from the cash and hard asset categories to fixed income investments. But he also needs to protect his retirement income from inflation. So he keeps the same amount of dollars in equities, plus maintains a small proportion of his money in hard assets.

Cash and cash equivalents	15 percent
Fixed-income vehicles	45 percent
Equities	30 percent
Hard assets	10 percent

Also, this allocation works not only in the two years prior to his retirement but also well into his retirement years.

What's next?

When it comes time to implement your allocation, you've got to decide how. Will you use a stock broker? a money manager? or will you use mutual funds and do the work yourself?

The answer depends primarily on the amount of money you have to invest and your personal preferences. One rule of thumb: opt for mutual funds if your investable assets add up to less than $50,000, a broker if your assets are between $50,000 and $250,000 and a money manager if your assets exceed $250,000.

Here's another concept you should know about: dollar cost averaging. Take a look at the charts that follow. They illustrate the benefits of this technique.

Dollar-cost averaging is a time-honored and simple method that calls for set dollars amounts to be invested at fixed intervals. You avoid buying investments at their

Let's assume you earmark $10,000 for this investment over the next 12 months. Furthermore, let's assume that you invest in $2,000 increments each quarter, as shown below:

	Up Market			Mixed Market			Down Market		
Date	*Investment Amount*	*Price Per Share*	*Shares Acquired*	*Investment Amount*	*Price Per Share*	*Shares Acquired*	*Investment Amount*	*Price Per Share*	*Shares Acquired*
Today	$ 2,000	$ 10	200	$ 2,000	$15	133	$ 2,000	$ 30	67
3 mos.	2,000	25	80	2,000	10	200	2,000	25	80
6 mos.	2,000	20	100	2,000	15	133	2,000	20	100
9 mos.	2,000	25	80	2,000	10	200	2,000	15	133
12 mos.	2,000	30	67	2,000	15	133	$ 2,000	$ 10	200
	$10,000	$110	527	$10,000	$65	799	$10,000	$100	580
	Average Share Cost $18.98 *($10,000/527)*		Average Share Price $22.00 *($110/5)*	Average Share Cost $12.52 *($10,000/799)*		Average Share Price $13.00 *($65/5)*	Average Share Cost $17.24 *($10,000/580)*		Average Share Price $20.00 *($100/5)*

peak price. Note that you inherently use dollar-cost averaging with some investments: IRAs, Keoghs, 401(k)s, and dividend reinvestment plans all call for set contributions at regular intervals.

20

Taking Your Money Out

If you're not one of the 39 million people who collect Social Security benefits now, chances are you're one of the 131 million who will pocket benefits one day. But Social Security won't start sending you monthly checks until you notify the local office that you're ready. How do you apply for Social Security benefits? That's what this chapter is all about.

How do you apply for benefits?

Uncle Sam requires you to file an application with your local Social Security Administration office. For more information, ask the Social Security Administration to send you a free copy of its Publication 05-10002,

What You Can Expect When You Visit a Social Security Office.

The toll-free number is (800) 234-5772.

When do you apply for benefits?

It's smart to apply for Social Security three months before you expect to begin receiving your benefits. That way, you won't have to wait for your check.

What information does the government require?

Uncle Sam requires you to prove your age.

So, when you apply for benefits, take along a certified copy of your birth certificate, hospital birth record, or baptismal certificate.

You'll also need your Social Security card, a copy of your most recent W-2 Form, or, if you're self-employed, a copy of your latest federal tax return.

If you're married and your spouse is applying for benefits too, have in hand his or her certified birth certificate or hospital record and his or her Social Security card. You'll also need a certified copy of your marriage certificate.

If you're divorced, take along your divorce papers.

When should you obtain these documents?

Most experts suggest you obtain the necessary documents early and check your earnings record—at least nine months before you expect to receive your first Social Security check.

How often are benefits paid?

Once a month, you'll receive your Social Security check. Uncle Sam mails the checks so you have your money by the third day of each month.

You may also request that your check be directly deposited to an account you designate. To do so, simply telephone your Social Security office. It will provide you with the necessary forms.

When can you collect benefits?

Uncle Sam says you're eligible to receive Social Security benefits when you retire. Members of your immediate family are also eligible for benefits when you retire. What are the rules? Let's take a look.

You're entitled to Social Security benefits when you retire, as long as you're sixty-two years of age or older. Likewise, a spouse who does not work outside the home is entitled to Social Security benefits, as long as he or she is aged sixty-two or older and you're already receiving benefits.

What if you retire and your spouse is caring for your minor child? Your spouse is entitled to receive Social Security benefits regardless of his or her age—but only as long as your child is under the age of sixteen or is disabled.

Your child may receive Social Security benefits, too, when you retire. But the child must be under the age of eighteen—or nineteen if he or she is in high school. If the child is disabled before age 22, he or she is entitled to receive benefits no matter what the age.

When should you start to collect benefits?

When you start to collect Social Security benefits—at age sixty-two or later—has an effect on how much you'll receive. For every month before age sixty-five that you begin receiving benefits, these benefits are reduced by $\frac{5}{9}$ of one percent.

So if you start collecting at age sixty-two, the youngest possible age, your check could be as low as 80 percent of the full benefit you would otherwise be entitled to receive (possibly as low as 70 percent of the full amount if you retire after 2021).

But for every month after you turn sixty-five that you

postpone collecting Social Security, the benefits go up. Future Social Security benefits increase by 3 percent a year for those who reach age sixty-five between 1982 and 1989—but only until age seventy.

What about those who reach age sixty-five in 1990 or later? They may get an increased benefit from 3½ percent to 8 percent a year, depending on how long after 1924 they were born. Here's an example. Say your annual benefit at age sixty-five adds up to $7,152. If you start collecting at age sixty-two, you receive only $5,722, a 20 percent reduction.

But if you wait until age sixty-six to collect benefits, your payment climbs to $7,367; at age sixty-seven, $7,588; and so on until the ceiling is reached at age seventy.

So, you ask, are you better off collecting your benefits at age sixty-two or waiting until you are sixty-five?

Most people are better off collecting their benefits at age sixty-two—assuming they don't continue to work and pocket in excess of the earnings limit. In fact, the only people who collect more over the long haul by waiting until they're sixty-five to receive benefits are those who live beyond age seventy-seven as is shown in the next chart.

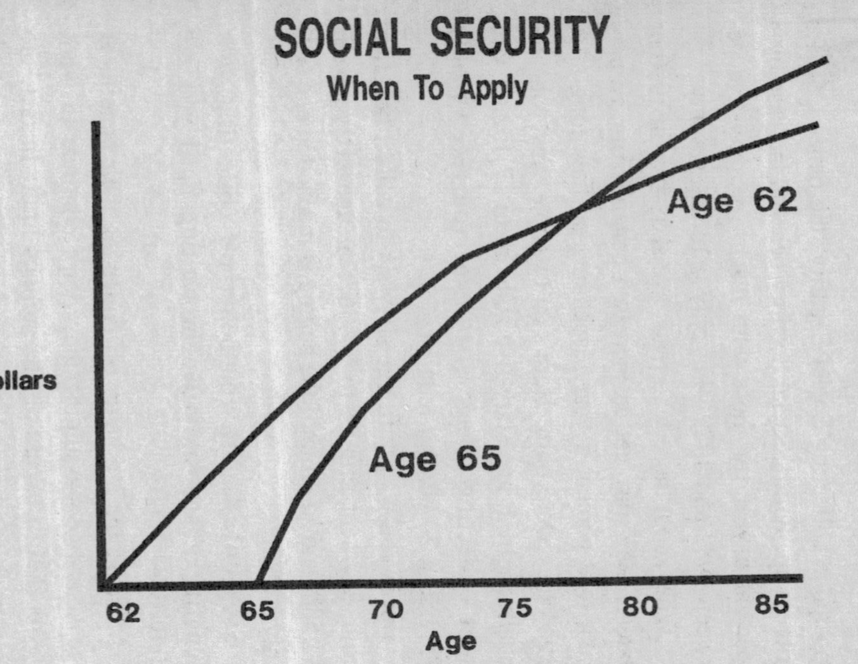
SOCIAL SECURITY
When To Apply
Age 62
Age 65
Dollars
62
65
70
75
80
85
Age

Will you and your spouse both receive benefits?

Say each of you is entitled to benefits because of your own earnings. In this case, you'll receive benefits independently of one another. But say your spouse has never worked outside the home. Then your spouse is eligible to collect a spousal benefit of between 37.5 percent and 50 percent of your benefits, depending on the age of each of you when you retire.

What if your spouse has worked outside the home? Then he or she may collect either a spousal benefit or his or her own benefit, whichever is greater.

Are your Social Security benefits taxed?

Uncle Sam requires that you include part of your Social Security benefits in your taxable income if your income tops a pre-set ceiling—$32,000 for married couples who file jointly, $25,000 for single people. Here are the rules.

If your adjusted gross income (AGI) plus one-half of your Social Security benefits exceeds the ceiling, a portion of your benefits are taxable. And for this calculation only, your AGI also includes any tax-exempt interest you've earned—from municipal bonds, say.

How much becomes taxable?

The taxable part is either one-half your benefits or

one-half the difference between your AGI and the ceiling, whichever is less.

Here's an example of how to do the calculation.

Say your AGI—including tax-exempt interest but before you add in your Social Security benefits—comes to $60,000. Your Social Security benefits total $9,048. You divide this number by two and get $4,524. For purposes of the taxability test, then, your income comes to $64,524 ($60,000 plus $4,524).

Since $64,524 is more than the base amount of $32,000, some part of your Social Security benefits is taxable. To figure how much, subtract the base amount—$32,000—from your income, which, for purposes of the taxability test, is $64,524. The result is $32,524.

Now, divide that amount by two to get $16,262. This amount—$16,262—is more than half your benefits—$4,524. So $4,524 of your benefits is taxable to you.

Can you lose retirement benefits by working?

You can lose all or part of your monthly benefits by becoming employed if: you're under age seventy but older than sixty-four, and your earnings from working exceed $9,360 in 1990; or you're under age sixty-five

for the full year and your earnings from employment top $6,840 in 1990.

The amount you lose depends on your age and how much your earnings top these ceilings. If you're under age sixty-five, you'll lose $1 in benefits for each $2 in earnings above the limits. If you're older than sixty-four but younger than seventy, you'll lose $1 for every $3 in excess earnings.

But in the first year you become eligible for benefits, a monthly test also applies. That way, you lose no benefits in this first year, because of the portion of the year that you worked.

For example, say, in 1990, you reached age sixty-five and retire. You'd receive full benefits for any month in which you earn less than $780 and aren't self-employed. This rule holds true regardless of your total earnings for the year.

If you're between the ages of sixty-two and sixty-four, you lose no benefits during your first year of retirement as long as your monthly earnings don't top $570. You should know that you can apply this monthly test only once in the first year you're eligible for Social Security. Again, this rule holds true regardless of your earnings for the year.

If you're earning more than you're allowed, call the

Social Security Administration and report the information to them. You'll probably find it less painful to receive less in benefits now than face having to pay back benefits that you weren't entitled to receive.

Moreover, if you intentionally fail to report your earnings or report them incorrectly, you'll pay a penalty. The penalty equals one or more months of lost benefits. In addition to the penalty, you must repay your excess benefits.

Keep in mind, though, that the earnings limitation doesn't apply once you reach seventy. You can then earn as much as you want without sacrificing any of your benefits.

Let's take a closer look at how working can cut into your benefits. Assume you're sixty-three years old and retired. You decide to work part-time to supplement your retirement income and earn $20,000 during the year.

Before you pat yourself on the back, consider these figures. You're in the 28-percent tax bracket, and Uncle Sam will take a hefty $5,600 (28 percent times $20,000) in federal taxes. Your Social Security taxes equal another $1,530 (7.65 percent times $20,000). Let's assume, as well, a state tax bite of 5 percent, or $1,000 (5 percent times $20,000).

Finally, you'll lose $6,580 in Social Security benefits

(50 percent times [$20,000 minus $6,840]). In other words, because of taxes and lost Social Security benefits, you take home only $5,290—or a mere 26 percent of your earnings.

Now that you know about collecting benefits from Social Security, we'll look in the next chapter at receiving money over time from your company retirement plan.

21

How to Make Annuities Pay

Sometimes you're given a choice when it comes to withdrawing money from a tax-deferred retirement plan. You may spread your withdrawals out over time—that is, receive them in the form of annuity—or you may pull out your funds all at once.

If you're allowed to choose, which is best for you? You should know that annuities and lump sum distributions are designed to be "actuarially equivalent." In other words, you're supposed to get the same amount of money in the end.

Annuities and lump sums are not equivalent if you die before or after the actuaries say you should. If you die sooner than your actuarial life expectancy, you're better off with a lump sum. If you die later, you're better off with an annuity.

Another consideration is the rate of return you'll get on your money. When you take an annuity, your company retirement plan takes responsibility for investing the money. So the investment risk is the company's—not yours. When you take a lump sum distribution, though, you assume responsibility for investing your retirement dollars, and you bear the investment risk.

The annuity payment is calculated assuming a particular investment rate of return. If you think you can beat this assumed rate of return, you may opt for a lump sum.

Finally, convenience may be an issue for you. Taking an annuity means you'll automatically receive a check each month. With a lump sum withdrawal, you'll have to arrange the amount and timing of your payments.

In this chapter, we'll cover annuities or payments over time, which is how most defined-benefit plans pay benefits. In the next chapter, we'll tell you what you need to know about lump-sum withdrawals, which are more common to defined-contribution plans.

What kinds of annuities are available?

You may not know it, but retirement plans usually offer employees a choice of several types of annuities. The first is a single life, which is an annuity spread over the life of the employee. If you're married, you may prefer to opt for what's known as a joint and survivor (J&S) annuity, which pays benefits to you and your spouse as long as either of you live.

Another kind of annuity is one that pays benefits for only a set number of years. For example, your employer might offer an annuity that pays a benefit for ten years after you retire. If you die before the ten years are up, your employer continues to make annuity payments to your spouse or designated beneficiary until the end of the ten-year period.

What type of annuity is best?

The answer varies for each individual and depends on a variety of circumstances—your marital status; the health and ages of you and your spouse at the time you retire; the financial resources available to your surviving spouse; and whether, if you're unmarried, you want to leave some of your retirement benefits to a beneficiary.

Let's look first at the choice between a single life annuity and a joint and survivor annuity first. You'll receive less money each month with a J&S annuity than you would with a single life annuity. The reason is that the dollars that are being annuitized are spread over a potentially longer period of time—over the course of two lives rather than one.

Still, if you and your spouse die when actuaries say you're supposed to, the total dollar amount is the same for both. In other words, single life and joint and survivor annuities are actuarially equivalent.

So should you choose a single life or a joint and survivor? A primary consideration is your health and the health of your spouse. If you think you're likely to die before your spouse does, a J&S annuity is probably your best bet. If your spouse is likely to die before you, you may want to opt for a single life annuity.

Another important consideration is whether your spouse has his or her own pension. If your surviving spouse doesn't need income from your annuity, choose a single life.

You may also have life insurance or other assets to provide income to your surviving spouse, which, again, makes a single life annuity attractive.

Under the law, if you opt for anything other than a 50 percent or higher J&S, your spouse has to give his or her consent, and this consent must be in the form of a notarized waiver that both you and your spouse have signed.

Wait a minute, you say. What's a 50 percent J&S?

Let's explain. Once you decide to opt for a joint and survivor annuity, you must decide between a 50 percent J&S and a 100 percent J&S or some variation in between. These percentages refer to the amount of the

monthly annuity payments that will continue after you die.

If your single life annuity is $600 a month, your surviving spouse or beneficiary gets nothing. With a 50 percent J&S option, your annuity is reduced, let's say, by 10% to $540 a month. Your surviving spouse receives $270 a month after you die. With a 100-percent J&S, your $540 annuity is reduced—by, say, $100—to account for the extra amount your spouse will receive after you die. Your surviving spouse would continue to receive your $440 a month annuity.

Which is best for you? Again, you should calculate whether you have enough life insurance or other assets to make up the loss your spouse would suffer if you opted for less than a 100-percent J&S. If you do, you may want to choose something less than a 100 percent J&S.

What is an excess distribution?

Uncle Sam imposes a 15 percent additional tax on so-called excess distributions. How do you know if you've received one?

Add up all the money you've collected this year from your tax-deferred retirement accounts, such as your pension, 401(k), IRA, and ESOP. However, exclude Social

Security benefits and any money that's a return of your after-tax contributions to a plan. Then, from this amount, subtract $150,000.

The result—meaning the amount that tops $150,000—is your excess distribution, unless, that is, you've withdrawn a lump-sum this year that was taxed under five-year averaging. (We'll detail lump-sum distributions and five-year averaging in the next chapter.) In that case, your excess distribution equals the lump-sum amount that tops $750,000.

Uncle Sam applies these excess distributions rules no matter at what age you withdraw your money—whether it's before or after age fifty-nine and a half.

Exempt are distributions that come from after-tax employee contributions and distributions that you roll over into an IRA or other qualified plan.

Our advice? If you think part of your retirement benefits will be subject to the 15 percent tax on excess distributions, you may want to take out some of your money early or roll it over into another account. In any event, ask your tax adviser for his or her assistance.

Now, on to lump-sum withdrawals.

22

The Latest on Lump-Sum Withdrawals

What's your alternative to receiving your retirement benefits over a period of time—that is, in the form of an annuity? It's a lump-sum withdrawal.

When it comes to lump-sum withdrawals, Uncle Sam gives you a choice. He says you can roll over the funds into an IRA and postpone paying taxes. Or, you can pay taxes now. You can also roll over part of your distribution—as long as it adds up to 50% or more—to an IRA and postpone taxes on the portion you've rolled over. All these choices have tax consequences.

What are they? In this chapter, we'll take a look.

What if you roll over your money to an IRA?

The law gives you 60 days to roll over your lump-sum distribution into an IRA or other tax-favored retirement account.

The advantages of rolling over your distribution? You're not taxed currently, and you get tax-deferred compounding of your money while it remains in the IRA.

What if you don't roll over your money to an IRA?

If you withdraw all the money out of your company pension plan in one lump and don't roll it over, the law allows you to use a device known as five-year forward averaging. And five-year averaging can work to your advantage.

Why? You may pay less tax. Although you receive the amount in one year, you calculate your tax as if you had withdrawn the money over five years.

The result: You pay all the tax at once for the year in which you receive your distribution. However, you may pay it at lower marginal rates.

Here's a simple example of how five-year averaging works.

Say the year is 1990, you're slated to retire in June,

you're married, and you opt to receive your $250,000 in retirement benefits in a lump sum.

You calculate your tax liability this way.

Total the amount of your lump-sum withdrawal—$250,000. Then divide this number by five—for five years. The result is $50,000. Now, with the tax-rate schedules, calculate the tax that a single person would pay, even though you're married, on $50,000. (The tax-rate schedule for 1990 follows).

Single Tax Rates for 1990	
$ 0 to $19,450	15%
19,451 to 47,050	28
47,051 to 97,620	33
97,621 or more	28

You multiply 15 percent times the first $19,450 to get $2,917.50. You then multiply 28 percent times your next $27,600 to get $7,728 and 33 percent times $2,950 to get $973.50. Your total tax, then, comes to $11,619.

After you've figured this amount, multiply it by five—again, for five years—to get the federal tax due on your $250,000 withdrawal—$58,095.

So will you save taxes with five-year averaging? You certainly will, and here's the reason. When you figure the tax you owe, you do so without regard to your other income.

That is, you compute the tax on your lump-sum withdrawal without adding it to your other income. That means, Uncle Sam taxes part of your retirement benefit at 15 percent. If you had to add your lump-sum withdrawal to all your other income, you'd end up paying taxes on all your income at the same rate as your last dollar of income, which is your highest marginal rate—28 percent, say.

Here's something else you should know. Uncle Sam gives you another break if you use five-year averaging and your lump-sum withdrawal comes to less than $70,000.

In this case, a portion of your withdrawal is tax-free. How much? Under the law, your maximum tax-free amount equals 50 percent of your lump-sum withdrawal—but no more than $10,000. This means if you collect a lump-sum distribution of $20,000, you may exclude $10,000 of that amount from taxation.

The rules say that for every dollar your lump-sum withdrawal tops $20,000, your tax-free amount drops by 20 cents. So if you take a $45,000 lump-sum withdrawal, you may exclude only $5,000 of that amount from taxation. And if you withdraw $70,000, you may not exclude one nickel.

Now, before you decide to opt for five-year averaging, you should know that the IRS attaches some strings to its generosity.

For starters, it says that you're entitled to use five-year averaging only once in your life and then only after you reach age fifty-nine and one-half.

What's more, not all lump-sum withdrawals qualify for five-year averaging. Which ones do and which don't? Let's take a look.

Under the rules, you must have participated in your retirement plan for five tax years before the tax year in which you pocket your lump-sum withdrawal. (The IRS will waive this rule, though, if the distribution is made because you have died.)

The rules also state that the amount you receive must equal the full amount due you from all plans of the same type—for example, profit-sharing-type plans, pension-type plans, and stock bonus-type plans. Moreover, you must receive the lump sum in a single calendar year.

Another requirement is that your lump-sum withdrawal is payable if you become disabled or die, or if your employment is terminated by you or your company.

What else do you need to know about lump sum withdrawals? When Congress enacted the five-year averaging rules in 1986, it gave taxpayers whose birthdays fall on December 31, 1935, or earlier, a choice; these people may use either five-year averaging or 10-year averaging.

There's only one catch. If you opt to use 10-year averaging, you must also use the 1986 tax-rate schedules to calculate the tax on your lump-sum withdrawal.

And here's another boon if your birthday falls on December 31, 1935, or earlier. You're entitled to use 10-year averaging if you take a lump-sum withdrawal prior to age 59½.

So, you ask, if you meet the age requirement, will you be better off—tax-wise—with five-year averaging or 10-year averaging?

As a rule of thumb, you pay less tax with 10-year averaging if your 1990 distribution comes to less than $473,700. The following table shows the effective tax rate on various distribution amounts under both five- and 10-year averaging elections.

Distribution	*10 year*	*5 year*
$ 20,000	5.5%	7.5%
50,000	11.7	13.8
100,000	14.5	15.4
200,000	18.5	21.7
300,000	22.1	24.9
400,000	25.7	26.9
500,000	28.7	28.0

Another benefit if you or your employer made contributions prior to 1974 and you qualify for 10-year averaging: Uncle Sam may consider part of your distribution to be a capital gain that will qualify for a special 20% rate.

Which option should you choose? Electing averaging or rolling over your money into an IRA?

The decision of when to receive your distribution and how to pay taxes on the funds depends on the size of the distribution, when you need the funds, and your personal financial situation. So you need to ask yourself three questions before making a decision.

First, are you going to need your retirement dollars in the near future? Say, for example, you need your lump sum to make a down payment on a piece of real estate. Then taking your lump sum distribution, electing special averaging and not rolling it over to an IRA is the better choice.

Second, do you plan to invest your lump sum to provide you with a long steady stream of income beginning at retirement or at some future date after you retire. In this case, an IRA rollover usually makes the most sense.

Third, do you need your lump sum at some future date to make a major purchase, again, buying real estate, say. In this case, your choice depends on when you need the funds. If you need them later rather than sooner, you may want to roll them over to an IRA for now. Then you can withdraw the money from your IRA when you need it.

Let's take a closer look at each of these situations.

What if you need the money for the near term?

If you have a near-term need for the funds, taking your lump sum distribution and electing five- or ten-year averaging is your best bet.

Once you place the funds into an IRA, you must pay taxes on any amounts you withdraw at regular tax rates. You don't have the advantage of the special averaging rules.

Also, if you take out money from an IRA in an amount that tops $150,000 annually, the amount you take out is subject to a 15 percent excise tax. However, if you elect five- or ten-year averaging, the ceiling is increased to $750,000 a year.

Here's an example that compares ten-year averaging with rolling over money to an IRA. We'll assume that total distribution comes to $250,000. You subtract your nondeductible contributions to the plan to get your total taxable distribution of $200,000. You would get an 8 percent return on your money if you placed it in an IRA. You would earn an after-tax return of 5.75 percent on non-IRA funds. Your tax bracket is 28 percent, and you're investing the money for one year.

	Averaging	*Rollover*
Total distribution	$250,000	$250,000
After-tax contributions	(50,000)	(50,000)
Taxable distribution	200,000	200,000
Tax (forward averaging)	36,924	0
Amount available to invest	$163,076	200,000
Invested at 5.75% / 8% for one year	$172,453	216,000
Less taxes payable on distribution	0	(70,380)*
Net amount available	172,453	145,620

* Include a 15 percent excise tax on the excess of $150,000

The following graph shows the lump sum available after investing for one, two, three, four, and five years. As you can see, the difference between the two options gets smaller the longer you invest the funds.

After-Tax Funds from a $200,000 Distribution

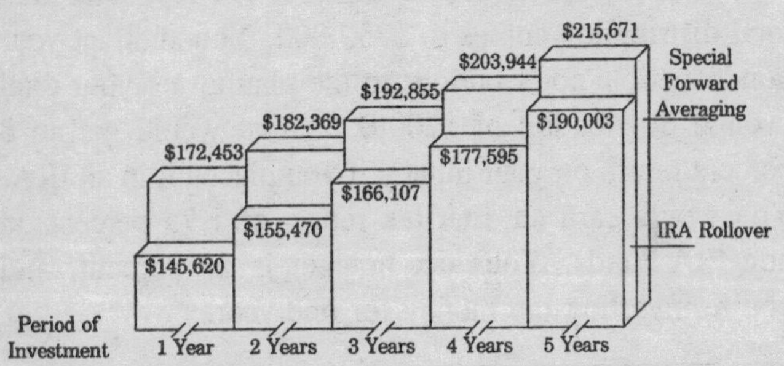

For example if you use ten-year averaging and invest a $200,000 distribution for one year, you'll have, after taxes, $172,453. With an IRA rollover, you'll have only $145,620. However, the situation is very different after five years. Then, if you opt for averaging and invest your $200,000, you'll end up with $215,671, whereas your IRA after-tax amount will equal $190,002.

What if you need the funds some time in the future?

You have a difficult decision to make if you'll need your retirement funds sometime in the future. This scenario assumes that you invest your dollars for some period of time, then withdraw them at a later date.

Initially, as we just saw, electing special averaging is more advantageous. At some point, however, rolling over the funds into an IRA would be more beneficial.

The deciding factors include: the length of time you'll leave the funds invested before you withdraw them; the rate of return you'll earn on the dollars you've invested; and your marginal federal and state income tax brackets at the time you ultimately withdraw your funds.

Say, for example, that your distribution adds up to $100,000, and you could earn 8 percent in an IRA and a taxable equivalent rate of 5.75 percent outside of an IRA.

Then your "crossover" point is about ten years. So if you need all your dollars in fewer than ten years, you would elect special averaging when you received the distribution. If you plan to invest the funds for more than ten years, you'd be better off rolling over your dollars to an IRA.

What if you need a steady stream of income?

If you want your retirement dollars to generate a stream of income for you throughout retirement, you're usually better off rolling the funds over into an IRA. Here's why. You're money isn't taxed currently, and your investment earnings continue to grow on a tax-deferred basis. These features of an IRA offset the reduced tax rates of special averaging.

Let's look at an example that illustrates a stream of income over 20 years. Again, we'll assume a taxable distribution of $200,000, but with a 9 percent return on the IRA funds and an after-tax return of 6.5 percent on the non-IRA funds. We'll assume a greater rate of return because of the longer-term payout.

	Averaging	*Rollover*
Total distribution	$250,000	$250,000
After-tax contributions	(50,000)	(50,000)
Taxable distribution	200,000	200,000
Tax (forward averaging)	36,924	0
Amount available to invest	$163,076	200,000
Monthly annuity paid out for 20 years	$1,216	$1,799
Less taxes due on each distribution		(504)
Net monthly annuity	$1,216	$1,295
Total distribution after 20 years	$291,840	$310,800

As you can see, you're better off rolling over your dollars to an IRA.

What if you have combined needs?

If you want a lump sum as well as a stream of income, you have to analyze your situation closely to determine which choice you should make.

And it's a good idea to ask your tax adviser to help you with the analysis. One solution may be to do a partial roll over. The amount rolled over is not currently taxed. You must pay taxes on the amount not rolled over and you may not use special averaging.

If you decide to roll over, how do you get your money out of an IRA? We'll cover that topic in the chapter that follows.

23

More Rules on IRAs

When it comes to withdrawing money from your IRA, Uncle Sam is strict. In fact, he imposes some special restrictions on IRA withdrawals.

In this chapter, we'll take a look.

What are the rules governing IRA withdrawals?

For one, Uncle Sam won't allow you to ease your tax burden by using five-year averaging when you take out money from your IRA. Instead, he says, you must pay taxes on the amount you withdraw—in the year you withdraw it—at the same rates as your ordinary income.

If you find yourself in this situation, here's a strategy to consider. Why not withdraw the money over a number of years, rather than all at once?

This tactic makes sense if you don't need the money all at once—say, you just need a little money to supplement your income from other sources. You should remember that the longer your funds stay in your IRA, the more valuable the tax deferral.

On the other hand, you may need your IRA money all at once. Our advice is to run the numbers so that you understand the tax implications of each of the options available to you.

TIP The rules say you're not required to begin withdrawing IRA dollars until you reach age 70½. And you may pull out your money—in any amount and at any time—without penalty once you reach age 59½. So take care to plan carefully.

Remember that you must ante up a 15-percent excise tax on so-called excess IRA distributions. And since IRA withdrawals aren't eligible for five-year averaging, the special $750,000 exemption isn't available.

Also, as you recall, if you want your IRA money before you reach age 59½ and you aren't disabled, you'll pay a penalty—10 percent of the taxable amount you withdraw.

Is there any way to avoid this penalty? You may, if you withdraw your money in the form of an annuity, or payments made at least once a year and spread out over your lifetime.

According to Uncle Sam, you must make sure that the

payments are of approximately equal amounts. And, you must base the payments on your life expectancy or the joint life expectancies of you and your beneficiaries. The IRS provides tables that outline life expectancies.

Here's an example of how it works. Say you're age fifty. According to the IRS tables, you have a life expectancy of 33.1 years. In your IRA, you've accumulated $100,000. So you may withdraw $8,679 annually (assuming an 8 percent interest rate) from the account without paying a penalty.

Once you start these withdrawals, you must continue to receive them for at least five years and at least until you reach age 59½. Otherwise, your distributions don't escape the early withdrawal penalty.

As we've mentioned, the IRS doesn't like late IRA withdrawals any more than early withdrawals. According to the rules, you must begin withdrawing your accumulated IRA funds before April 1 of the year following the year you reach age 70½.

The amount you're required to take out depends on either your own life expectancy or—if you prefer—the joint life expectancies of you and your beneficiary.

What happens if you fail to pull out the required amount? Your mistake will cost you in the form of a hefty penalty. You'll pay a penalty that comes to 50 percent of the difference between the amount you pulled out and the amount the law said you should take out.

Consider this example. You are age 70½, and the IRS tables say that, based on your life expectancy, you must withdraw at least $6,000 annually from your IRA. But, in 1990, you compute the amount incorrectly and take out only $3,000.

Uncle Sam says you must ante up 50 percent of the difference between the amount you withdrew—$3,000—and the amount you were required to withdraw—$6,000. So you'll cough up a penalty of $1,500—that is, 50 percent times $3,000.

TIP You may reduce the amount of required withdrawals from your IRA by naming a younger person—your child, for example—as your beneficiary. If you do, your joint life expectancy will be quite long. So you'll be required to withdraw much less from your IRA account than you otherwise would.

Uncle Sam imposes some restrictions when you name a younger person as your beneficiary. If you do so, you'll need the help of your financial adviser.

So should you wait to withdraw your IRA dollars until you reach age 70½?

The rule of thumb is to keep your money in your IRA until age seventy and one half if you can. That way, earnings on your retirement dollars continue to compound tax-deferred.

But this rule of thumb doesn't always hold true. Say, for example, that you leave your dollars in your IRA until you reach age 70½. Then you begin to withdraw them. Your annual payments—based on your life expectancy—top $150,000.

That means you're subject to the 15 percent excise tax. In your case, you'd be better off withdrawing your money earlier to avoid the excise tax.

What if you're younger than age 70½? You need to take into account not only the amount that's deposited in your IRA, but also the earnings on those dollars. Say, for example, that you're 60 years old and your IRA, which includes the amounts you've rolled over from your company retirement plans, adds up to $700,000. If those dollars grow at the rate of 8% a year, until you reach age 70½, your account will be worth nearly $1.6 million.

That means, your annual required withdrawal could top the floor for the excise tax, currently $150,000.

Now you know how to take your money out of retirement plans. In the next section, we'll look at how you can protect yourself financially should you become ill. We'll begin with Medicare.

24

All About Medicare

As an employee, most of your health-care expenses were covered by your company-provided health insurance program. But now that you're retired who pays?

Uncle Sam, for starters. Medicare—the $96-billion-a-year, federally-sponsored, national health insurance program—is your first line of defense.

Next comes, your company post-retirement medical insurance plan—if you're lucky enough to have one—or a health insurance policy that you've bought yourself.

Last is Medicaid, the government medical insurance program for those who, after having exhausted their financial resources, are unable to pay for health care.

In this chapter, we'll give you the lowdown on Medicare. We'll explain not only what Medicare pays for but, equally important, what it doesn't.

We'll begin, though, with a few basics.

What is Medicare?

First enacted in 1965, Medicare is actually two programs—not one. Medicare Part A helps pay when you're hospitalized or in a skilled nursing home. Medicare Part B helps cover your doctor bills and the expense of most other outpatient services.

Who is eligible for Medicare?

Almost anyone who's 65 years of age or older and entitled to Social Security benefits is automatically eligible for Medicare. In other words, you—as a wage earner—are entitled to Medicare benefits, just as you are to Social Security benefits, and so is your spouse. However, if you're not entitled to Social Security benefits, you can still enroll but you must pay an additional premium of $175 per month.

How do you apply for Medicare?

You apply for Medicare no later than three months before you turn age 65—even if you haven't retired and are still covered by your company health insurance.

When does Medicare coverage begin?

Medicare coverage begins on the first day of the month you reach age 65. And it makes no difference whether you're retired or still working.

What does Medicare Part A cover?

As we said, Medicare Part A pays when you're hospitalized or in a skilled nursing home—but only if five conditions, all prescribed by law, are met.

One, you're eligible for Medicare coverage. *Two*, a doctor orders your hospitalization. *Three*, the care you require is available only in a hospital.

Four, the hospital participates in the Medicare system. That is, it agrees to accept the amount it receives from Medicare as payment in full for the services it renders.

Five, the hospital's so-called utilization review or peer-review committees agree that you need hospital care. These committees are comprised of physicians who practice at the hospital and review cases to see that everyone who's hospitalized really requires the care they're receiving.

The inpatient services that Medicare Part A covers include: a semi-private room; all meals; regular nursing; use of special facilities, such as operating and recovery rooms, anesthesia, and intensive care; hospital-furnished drugs; and most blood transfusions.

Also covered: hospital-billed x-ray and other radiology services; medical supplies, such as casts; use of appliances, such as wheelchairs; and rehabilitation therapy.

When it comes to skilled nursing homes, Medicare pays only if the services you receive are "medically necessary" and a direct result from a hospitalization. Also, they must be provided in a "skilled" facility—one that meets Medicare's requirements—and in a home that's Medicare-approved.

You may not know it, but most nursing homes don't provide skilled care, and most skilled-care nursing homes aren't Medicare-approved.

Also, most people with long-term health problems, such as Alzheimer's disease, need custodial—not skilled—care, and Medicare doesn't pay for custodial care at all.

Does Medicare Part A cover home health care?

It does, but only under certain conditions. For example, the care must be prescribed by a physician, who, in turn, sets up a home health plan for you. Also, your care must require intermittent skilled nursing care or physical

or speech therapy, and you must be confined to your home.

In these cases, Medicare covers the cost of services such as part-time or intermittent skilled nursing care, speech, physical therapy, and occupational therapy.

How much does Medicare Part A pay?

For the first 60 days, Medicare usually pays all your hospital charges—as long as they don't top the approved amounts—after you subtract a $592 annual deductible in 1990. For the next 30 days, you pay $148 a day and Medicare covers the rest. If you have questions about how much Medicare Part A will pay in a particular situation, contact your local Social Security office. They should be able to help.

What does Medicare Part B cover?

Medicare Part B pays your doctor bills, plus services provided at your doctor's office, such as services of the office nurse, drugs you aren't able to administer yourself, transfusions, medical supplies, and physical, occupational, and speech therapy.

Part B also covers the cost of hospital outpatient services, such as emergency room and outpatient clinics, lab tests, radiological services, and medical supplies.

How much does Medicare Part B pay?

Part B covers 80 percent of your doctor bills and most other outpatient costs that don't top what the government calls *approved amounts*. Again, if you have questions about what Medicare Part B will pay in a specific situation, contact your local Social Security office.

What is an approved amount?

It's the price for services that Medicare deems standard in your city or town or other geographic area—$40 for a doctor visit, say.

If your doctor charges more than the approved amount, you or your insurance carrier must pay any excess charges over the approved amount. Say the year is 1990, and you live in Des Moines, Iowa, where the approved amount for an office visit with a doctor is $26. Your physician charges $38.50.

You or your private insurance carrier must fork over $17.70—that is, 20 percent of the approved amount or

$5.20, plus $12.50 (the difference between $26 and $38.50).

If you'd like to know the names of doctors in your area that charge no more than the approved amount, you can consult your local *Medicare Participating Physician/Supplier Directory*, a government publication that's available at your local Social Security office.

What is a co-payment?

With Part B, you're required to pay out of your own pocket 20 percent of the cost of services you receive. This unreimbursed amount is known as the co-payment.

What is Medigap?

Medigap plans are plans that you buy from private insurance carriers. They pay medical expenses not covered by Medicare.

Insurance carriers offer two types of Medigap policies. Most are of the first type, paying only your share of costs covered by Medicare.

The second—and more valuable type of Medigap policy—pays excess charges for doctor bills and lab tests, the charges that top Medicare's approved amounts.

Although these policies are usually no more costly

than the first type, they may require that you have an above-average medical history.

The cost of Medigap policies range from $400 to $1,200 a year, but you should know that a higher price tag doesn't always translate into better coverage.

If you'd like more information on Medigap plans, write to the Health Insurance Institute of America (Box 41455, Washington, DC 20018) and ask for a copy of *The Consumer's Guide to Medicare Supplemental Insurance*. It's free for the asking.

What does Medicare cost you?

Medicare Part A is provided to you by Uncle Sam if you're eligible for Social Security. Part B is optional, and you pay a monthly premium that's adjusted annually for inflation. In 1990, the Part B premium came to about $28.60. In addition, you're subject to a $75 annual deductible on services.

Although Part B is optional, most everyone will want to purchase it. That's because most company retirement plans assume that you've elected Part B coverage, and won't pay for medical expenses normally covered by Part B.

Also, if you don't enroll for Part B when you become

eligible but wait several years, you'll pay higher premiums. The premiums go up 10 percent for each 12 months that you're not enrolled.

What if you're still employed?

After you retire or reach age 65, Medicare becomes your primary insurer. Your employer's medical plan pays only those expenses not covered by Medicare.

What is Medicaid?

Medicaid is the medical program that was originally designed for poor people of all ages, and it provides a safety net of sorts for retirees—but only those in the most dire situations.

Most often, retirees rely on Medicaid to cover the cost of custodial care. In fact, the Brookings Institution estimates that 58 percent of all nursing-home patients are on Medicaid—or will be before they die—even though most weren't on welfare when they entered the homes.

Who qualifies for Medicaid?

You're eligible for Medicaid if your health-care costs absorb almost all of your income, and you've used up all but $1,000 to $4,000 of your assets—the exact amount varies by state. (Your financial adviser will know the rules in your state.)

What if your spouse is in a nursing home?

If your spouse is in a nursing home and the costs are being covered by Medicaid, you're usually allowed to receive no more than $1,500 a month in income and to hold onto only half of your combined assets up to $60,000, excluding the equity in your home.

Here's a strategy that enables you to qualify for Medicaid and preserve your assets for your heirs: Transfer title to your assets to family members other than your spouse or to a so-called Medicaid trust, which an attorney will prepare for about $1,000.

A Medicaid trust is simply a type of irrevocable living trust. You must place your assets in this trust more than 30 months before you apply for Medicaid.

Also, you and your spouse may serve as trustees of the trust, but the trust must prevent you from ever using the assets for your own benefit.

What if you wait to put your assets into a trust until you apply for Medicaid? In that case, you must pay for the first 30 months of care out of your own pocket. Then Medicaid takes over. If you wait to set up a trust, buy

enough long-term care insurance to cover the first 30 months of care.

Where can you learn more?

If you'd like more information on Medicare, ask the Department of Health and Human Services to send you copies of its booklets, *A Brief Explanation of Medicare*, *Your Medicare Handbook*, *Medicare/Medicaid—Which is Which*, and *How to Fill Out a Medicare Claim Form*.

You can obtain copies of these free publications by calling Medicare (the toll-free number is 800/888-1998) or writing the Department of Health and Human Services, Health Care Financing Administration, Baltimore, MD 21207.

Also available free of charge is *Information on Medicare and Health Insurance for Older People*. All you need to do is write the American Association of Retired Persons (1909 K St., NW, Washington, DC 20049) and ask for a copy.

[illegible] however, the [illegible]
[illegible] months of care.

Where can you learn more?

Request the [illegible] booklet on Medicare [illegible] the Department of Health and Human Services [illegible] copy of its booklet, *A Brief Explanation of Medicare* [illegible] *Medicare Handbook* [illegible] and [illegible]. [illegible] Department of Health and Human Services [illegible] MD 21207.

[illegible] Medicare and Health Insurance for Older People. [illegible] Washington, DC 20049 [illegible] for a copy.

[illegible]

25

Why Long-Term Care Insurance?

The longer you live, the greater the chance that you'll need long-term care insurance. And more of us are living longer. Since 1940, the odds of living to age 85 have doubled—from one in five to two in five, and they're expected to jump to three in five by the year 2030.

With longevity has come a new set of health problems.

In fact, some 30 percent of Americans who are eighty-five years of age or older now reside in nursing homes. Another 20 percent or so require home care—that is, they receive regular assistance from nurses, housekeepers, or meal-delivery services.

Where once the inability to care for oneself resulted primarily from cancer or other acute diseases, it's now more likely to come gradually.

People live for years with Alzheimer's disease and other chronic ailments that don't require long hospital stays, but leave their victims increasingly helpless.

In the old days, long-term care was the responsibility of children, but these days the givers of care are more likely to be paid strangers than family members. What do you need to know when it comes to long-term care insurance? You'll find out in this chapter.

Why long-term-care insurance?

The cost of providing long-term care to someone is an expense that can leave you financially crippled. And sometimes not even Medicare helps. You may not know it, but Medicare doesn't pay the medical bills of people who retire before age 65.

Also, most people think Medicare will pick up their nursing-home bills, but it won't. Medicare pays only for stays in so-called skilled nursing homes—and then only if admission follows a hospital stay. Further, Medicare coverage is limited to 100 days per admission.

What's more, when Medicare pays, it covers only about 50 percent of your actual health-care costs, leaving you to come up with the rest.

Nursing homes—on average—charge as much as $24,000 a year for their services, and the fees are rising at a rate that's higher than inflation. Home-care services, which include physical therapy, administration of drugs, and food preparation, are running upwards of $30 to $50 a day.

If you're like most people, you can't afford these expenses. A congressional subcommittee on aging recently found that between 70 percent and 80 percent of nursing-home residents had depleted all their assets in a year or so and were forced onto Medicaid.

Once poverty stricken, nursing-home patients often have to move to less desirable accommodations in the same institution or to a less expensive facility.

How do you protect yourself?

If you're 60 years of age or older and in good health, here's a way you can cover all your health-care needs. Spend the rest of your life in one of the nation's 800 so-called continuing-care or life-care retirement communities.

Residents of these communities get private apartments plus services such as housekeeping, meals, and medical care, including nursing-home care, on an as-needed basis.

Some communities charge a flat fee for entrance—usually $35,000 to $100,000, depending on the size of your apartment—and $500 to $2,000 a month for maintenance, meals, and health care. You then get whatever services you require at no additional cost.

Other communities charge less—typically entrance fees of $25,000 to $85,000 and $500 to $800 a month—but residents must pay extra for services beyond the minimum specified in their contracts, so read the fine print before you sign on the dotted line.

For instance, a contract might limit home health care to 60 days or require residents to pay 80 percent of the cost of care in the community's nursing home. Communities with the lowest entrance and monthly fees—$20,000 to $60,000 and $500 to $700—charge extra for each service.

Most fees are all-inclusive, but if you move to a community with separate fees for all or some services, you may still need medigap and long-term care insurance. These policies are sometimes offered at group rates to residents. You can save as much as 15 to 25 percent.

Increasingly, entrance fees at continuing-care communities are at least partially refundable if you change your mind at any time after you sign your contract. Also, some communities refund all or part of the entrance fees to the estate upon a resident's death.

It's wise to check the reputation of a facility you're

considering. You can do so by writing the attorney general of the state where the community is located.

Another indicator of sound management is accreditation by the American Association of Homes for the Aging (AAHA), a trade group based in Washington, D.C. But accreditation is voluntary, and only about seventy communities have met AAHA standards so far.

For a free list of accredited facilities, write the American Association of Homes for the Aging, 1129 20th St., NW, Washington, DC 20036. The group also publishes a guide on how to choose a continuing-care community. It's available for $4.

How else can you protect yourself from the cost of long-term care?

You can join a health maintenance organization that includes long-term care among its prepaid services. Or you can buy your own long-term care insurance policy. Buying long-term care insurance is the easiest alternative for most people.

But whether you should sign up for long-term-care insurance depends largely on your age. People under the age of fifty are best advised to do nothing. Why? Many retirement planning experts believe broader and better solutions, public or private, probably lie ahead. However, others argue that buying policies when you're under the age of 50 and locking in lower rates makes good sense.

When do benefits begin?

Some policies require hospitalization for three days before benefits begin. Yet, the need for care is often the result of a deteriorating condition such as arthritis, which may not put you in the hospital at all. The best policies require only that a doctor certify the need for care.

What do these policies cover?

Some people require medical services. Others just need personal care. Some people can get along in their own home. Others have to be in a nursing home.

Ideally, a long-term-care policy should offer the widest possible options, including nursing homes in three categories of medical care: skilled homes; intermediate homes, which provide rehabilitative therapy; and custodial homes, which offer little more than practical nursing.

The best policies also pay for care at home, adult

day-care centers and brief intermittent care at a nursing home, also known as respite care.

The policy should offer those benefits in nearly equal amounts. A policy that covers nursing-home care for years but home care for only a month or so forces you to opt for institutionalization or to skip benefits.

The fewer the types of care covered and the more heavily the choice is skewed toward one type of care, the less useful the policy is.

Most companies now cover home care, but some charge extra for it or reduce payments over time. Some plans pay for home care only after you've been in a nursing home for a period of time and then only for as many days as you were there.

What is excluded?

Alzheimer's disease can leave victims helpless for fifteen years or longer. That's why some insurers exclude Alzheimer's disease from the conditions their policies cover and why you shouldn't buy any such policy.

Most policies have a six-month waiting period before they start paying benefits for preexisting conditions. This clause is standard, and you can't avoid it.

What are the drawbacks of these policies?

Almost all policies have one major drawback: They indemnify you for a fixed dollar amount per day, no matter how much you're paying for services.

In contrast, hospital and major-medical insurance pays all or a high percentage of each bill. (One Blue Cross group policy in Rochester, New York, available to the public is an exception: It pays 75 percent of prevailing rates for long-term care.)

Can you renew your policy?

You can, if your policy is guaranteed renewable.

If you live in Arizona, Hawaii, Indiana, Iowa, Kansas, Nebraska, North Carolina, North Dakota, Oklahoma, or Virginia, count yourself lucky.

Your state law forbids insurance carriers from cancelling your long-term-care policy because of either your age or deteriorating health. Any policy that can cut you off just as your liability begins to increase is a rotten deal.

So make sure your coverage will continue for as long as you want it to and that your premiums can't be hiked unless everybody's are in your situation.

How much does long-term care insurance cost?

Annual premiums for long-term-care insurance range from $100 or so for those in their thirties to more than $3,000 for the broadest coverage on people nearing eighty.

Will your premiums rise?

Once you become insured, your premium should remain constant, unless it includes an inflation adjustment. In this case, your premium will rise with inflation.

Do these policies include a deductible?

How many days of care come out of your pocket before your benefits begin and how long they continue will greatly influence the premium you pay. Most insurers offer at least two choices of waiting periods—typically, anywhere from 20 days to 100 days.

Selecting a 100-day waiting period can reduce your premium by as much as 30 percent. So you probably want to choose as long a waiting period as you can afford.

At the other end, though, more is worth paying for. Since the majority of policyholders will need care for less than a year, benefits that quit after one year or so may cost only half as much as those continuing for the six-year maximum many policies currently offer.

The extra coverage, however, can mean the difference between solvency and bankruptcy for the minority whose confinement continues for years.

Who sells long-term care insurance?

About seventy commercial insurers and seven Blue Cross plans now offer coverage for long-term care in either a nursing home or the patient's own dwelling. Because the coverage is fairly new, insurers are wary of assuming too much risk.

Even the few plans offering reasonable and affordable protection aren't available in every state. Also, coverage is usually limited for a period of six years.

If you'd like the names of companies that sell long-term care insurance in your state, write the Health Insurance Association, 1001 Pennsylvania Ave., NW, Washington, DC 20004. The information is free for the asking.

Where can you write for more information?

A free brochure and shoppers' worksheet called *Choice Time* is available from Aetna Insurance (Box

104, Hartford, CT 06156). It was prepared by Esther Peterson, the dean of consumer advocates and the nation's first special assistant to the President for consumer affairs. In the Appendix you'll find a checklist to help you evaluate various policies.

26

What You Need To Know About Estimated Taxes

Now, most of us pay taxes the easy way—through payroll withholding. And unless you report substantial amounts of unearned income—dividends, interest, and so on—you aren't required to make estimated income tax payments to the government.

But that situation is likely to change once you retire. Like your self-employed friends, you'll face not one tax due date, April 15, but four—the fifteenth days of April, June, and September of the current year and the fifteenth of January of the following year.

On these days, you'll have to pony up estimated tax payments to the federal government—and probably to your state governments as well.

How much will you owe? The answer depends on your income. Some people don't realize that—depending on their income level—up to half their Social Security benefits may be taxable. (See chapter 20 for the details.) Also, pensions are taxable, and so are withdrawals from your IRA—unless, of course, you made nondeductible contributions to your IRA. So you must remember to add in these amounts when you figure your estimated tax.

What happens if you don't make these quarterly payments or don't ante up enough? You'll pay a penalty, which, by the way, you won't be able to deduct.

So if you plan to retire soon, it's important that you know the estimated tax rules. That's what this chapter is all about.

How much do you pay?

Uncle Sam doesn't care if he gets his money through payroll withholding, estimated taxes, or some combination of the two. But, as you might expect, he does care about getting his due. Moreover, he expects to collect on his timetable, not yours.

What if you retire, then take another salaried position? Or what if you're married and your spouse collects a regular paycheck?

If you or your spouse don't have enough taxes withheld from those paychecks, you'll have to ante up the difference in the form of estimated tax payments.

The rules say that you must fork over—through payroll withholding or estimated taxes or a combination of both—the lesser of 90 percent of your current year's tax bill or 100 percent of last year's tax.

When are estimated taxes due?

Uncle Sam wants his money four times a year. No excuses. The due dates for these estimated tax payments, as we mentioned, are April 15, June 15, September 15, and January 15.

What happens if the due date falls on a Saturday, Sunday, or legal holiday? In that case, you get a break. The IRS considers your payment on time if you make it on the next business day.

The postmark on the envelope is the date the IRS uses. Here's something else you should know: Your envelope must be postmarked by the U.S. Postal Service, not a private postage meter.

TIP Some people are nervous about the reliability of the U.S. mails. If you're one of them, send your check by registered or certified mail.

Your receipt will give you proof that you forwarded your estimated tax payment as the law requires.

What happens, you may ask, if you plan to ask for an extension to file your Form 1040? Does that mean you can also postpone your first estimated tax payment?

Unfortunately, the answer is no. It doesn't matter whether you requested an extension or filed your return on time. Your first estimated payment is still due April 15.

Can you skip payments?

Uncle Sam lets you skip your January estimated tax payment on one condition: You file your return and pay your tax liability in full on or before January 31.

He also lets you skip quarterly payments if your estimated tax bill for the year—after subtracting any taxes your employer withheld—comes to less than $500.

Finally, he says, you can skip quarterly payments if you owed no tax the previous year. In this case, you must be a U.S. citizen or resident for all of the past 12 months.

How do you calculate your payments?

Remember, the law says that your four quarterly payments must equal either 100 percent of the tax you paid the previous year—that is, the amount shown on your last year's return—or 90 percent of the tax you'll owe in the current year.

In other words, Uncle Sam gives you a choice, which can work to your advantage. How? Here's an example. Say your federal tax liability last year totaled $15,000.

This year, you expect to collect more in dividends than you did last year and estimate that your tax will come to $20,000. So how much should you pay to the IRS in quarterly payments this year?

Under the rules, you may send Uncle Sam either $15,000, the amount you paid last year, or $18,000, which is 90 percent of the $20,000 you estimate you'll owe this year.

Naturally, you choose the $15,000 option.

Wait a minute, you say. I know what my total payment must be, but what about each individual payment? Here are the rules.

Each of your quarterly payments must equal or exceed 25 percent of either 100 percent of last year's tax bill or 90 percent of the current year's tax bill.

What if you underpay?

If you underpay your estimated taxes, Uncle Sam will slap you with—you guessed it—an underpayment penalty. This penalty is levied on the amount you fall short. The amount of the penalty climbs or falls with current interest rates. As of the second quarter of 1990, you'd pay 11 percent on the shortfall.

How do you know if you've underpaid?

The rules say you've underpaid—and you'll be slapped with a penalty—when any single quarterly payment falls short, even if you make up the shortfall in your next payment. This rule holds true even if you ultimately pocket a tax refund when you file your Form 1040.

Say you underpay each of your first three estimated tax payments. Uncle Sam starts the penalty clock on each underpayment on the date the installment was due, and it ends when the underpayment is paid up.

How do you reduce the underpayment penalty?

Here's a way to put a cap on the underpayment penalty. Say it's time to make your fourth and last estimated payment for the year. You fork over to the IRS what you

owe on the fourth installment, plus the amount you underpaid on the first three installments.

You've stopped the penalty clock cold. You still owe a penalty—the size of which depends on current interest rates—but the penalty is no longer accruing.

Here's another idea for eliminating the penalty entirely. You can use this strategy if you're still drawing a salary that's subject to tax withholding.

Just file a new Form W-4, "Employee's Withholding Allowance Certificate," with your employer and claim fewer or even no allowances. Your employer will then withhold an extra amount. That way, you can make up the shortfall from your underpayment of estimated taxes.

This strategy works, because the government totals all your payroll withholding over the year and divides the amount by four. Of course, if you're married and file jointly and your spouse is still collecting a paycheck, you can have him or her ask that extra money be withheld.

That way, too, you can avoid an underpayment penalty.

Keep in mind, though, that any additional payroll withholding must be done before the end of the tax year. Otherwise, you aren't off the penalty hook.

What if you borrow to make your estimated payments?

If you take out a loan to make your estimated tax payments, Uncle Sam won't allow you to deduct the interest you pay on the money you borrow. Why? He classifies the interest as personal interest, and personal interest isn't deductible at all beginning in 1991.

TIP It's probably a mistake to borrow money simply to avoid the underpayment penalty. Here's the reason. It's difficult in today's market to borrow money at an interest rate that's less than the 11 percent used to determine the underpayment penalty.

What if you overpay your taxes?

Uncle Sam gives you a choice when it comes to overpayments. He says you may apply the overpayment to the amount of taxes you'll owe next year or pocket a refund.

If your overpayment is almost the same as the amount you'll owe when you make your first estimated tax installment, it makes sense to apply the overpayment to your first installment. Why write a check to cover an amount that the IRS already has in hand?

What if the amount you overpaid adds up to a good

deal more than you'll owe in the first and even second quarter? You should pay your first and second quarter installments from the overpayment, then request that Uncle Sam refund the rest.

Also, if you think your income will drop significantly this year and you expect to pay little or no estimated tax, ask for a refund of the overpayment when you file your 1040.

Why? The rules say that you can't change your mind once you've requested that the IRS apply your overpayment to your estimated tax.

There's another important tax issue that might confront you when you enter retirement: the tax ramifications of selling your home. That's the subject we'll address in our next chapter.

27

Tax-Wise Ways to Sell Your Home

One of the best ways for house-rich retirees to extract cash from their homes is to trade down—that is, sell their present house for one that costs less. This strategy enables them to slash living expenses plus convert some equity into a lump sum that they can invest for income.

In this chapter, we'll tell you what you need to know to squeeze the maximum return from your prime asset—and minimize your tax bill.

Let's start, though, with a few quick definitions. We think you'll find them useful, because we use these terms frequently in this chapter.

What is a residence?

An obvious question, you say, but not to the authors of the Internal Revenue Code. A residence—in the eyes of these tax writers—is a place that includes basic living accommodations. So houses, apartments, condominiums, and mobile homes qualify as residences, and so do houseboats.

What is a principal residence?

A principal residence is the home where you spend most of your time. In other words, it's your primary residence. Just owning a house doesn't make it your principal residence. The rules say you must actually live in that house for it to qualify as your primary residence.

The IRS sets no limits on the amount of time you must spend in your home for it to be considered your principal residence, but we suggest you use common sense.

What if your home doesn't qualify as your primary residence? You're not entitled to the tax breaks Uncle Sam provides to homeowners.

What is your adjusted selling price?

It's the sum you receive from the sale of your home—that is, the sales price less your selling costs—minus any fixing-up expenses.

What are fixing-up expenses?

They're costs you incur getting your home ready to sell. Ordinarily, you don't profit—tax-wise, at least—when you fix up your house. Uncle Sam won't let you write off the cost of, say, painting or wallpapering on your Form 1040.

Nor does he allow you to subtract these expenses directly from your gain when you sell. But these costs do help slash your gain. That's because you subtract them from your selling price to get your adjusted selling price.

☞ CAUTION Fixing-up expenses are for repair and maintenance—not for improvements. (We'll explain the difference shortly.) Also, you must do the fixing up during the 90 days before you sign the papers to sell your house, and you must pay for the repairs within 30 days after the sale. Otherwise, you may not subtract them.

What is a direct selling expense?

It's an expense, such as the commission you pay a real estate agent, that you subtract directly from the gain on your house.

What is an improvement?

In the eyes of Uncle Sam, it's anything that adds to your home's value or appreciably prolongs its life. Adding a room, installing central air conditioning, and putting up new gutters count as improvements. And so do less obvious costs, such as installing venetian blinds.

What is your basis?

Your basis is the cost of your home plus the cost of any improvements you've made (but not fixing-up expenses). Your basis also includes some of the costs you incurred when you purchased your house and while you owned it—for example, attorneys' fees, appraisal fees, costs of defending title to the property, costs of title search and insurance, fees for the recording of the deed and mortgage, late closing charges, and survey expenses.

How do you calculate your gain?

It's simple. All you need do is subtract your basis from your selling price. Then subtract your fixing-up expenses. Here's an example.

Say the original cost of your home was $50,000. Your appraisal fees, attorney's fees, and other purchasing expenses added up to $2,000. Over the years, you've added a new bathroom for $9,000 and installed central air conditioning and heating for $3,000.

Now, say you sell your old homestead for a hefty $90,000; your broker's commission and other selling expenses come to $5,000.

Is your gain $40,000—that is, your $90,000 sale price less your $50,000 cost? Definitely not. As we've seen, you calculate your gain by adding your purchasing expenses and the cost of improvements to your basis, then subtracting your selling expenses from the sales proceeds.

So in our example, your cost basis comes to $64,000—that is, your $50,000 original cost plus $14,000 in improvements and purchasing expenses.

The amount you pocket after you subtract your selling expenses—$5,000 broker's commission—is $85,000. So your gain is $21,000—that is, $85,000 minus $64,000.

Do you pay taxes on your gain?

When it comes to selling your home, Uncle Sam is no Scrooge. He allows you to defer paying income taxes on your gain if you meet two simple conditions.

One, you must buy or build and occupy a new principal residence within 24 months before or after the date you sell your old home.

Two, you must buy or build your new principal residence for an amount that equals at least the adjusted selling price of your old home.

That means, of course, that if you intend, as many retirees do, to buy a less expensive home or rent, you may have to pay taxes. We'll get to that situation in a moment, Let's assume for now, however, that you meet the two conditions. What else do you need to know?

Let's return to our previous example.

You pay no tax on your $21,000 profit as long as you purchase or build a new home that costs $85,000 or more—or at least you don't pay any tax now. Here's what we mean.

Say you buy a new house for $86,000. Your purchasing costs add up to $4,000. That means your basis in your new home is $90,000 ($86,000 plus $4,000). Right?

Wrong. Under the rules, you must reduce your basis in your new home by the amount of gain from your old house that you rolled over or deferred. That means your basis in your new home adds up to only $69,000—that is, $86,000 plus $4,000 minus the $21,000 gain you deferred.

Now, suppose it's a year later, and you decide to tour the world for two years. You sell your home for $90,000, but decide not to buy a new one.

Uncle Sam requires you to report on your Form 1040 the difference between your selling price—$90,000—and your basis, $69,000. And—and this is the bad news—your gain of $21,000 is now taxable, since you didn't buy or build a new principal residence.

What if you had purchased another house? You'd still be in hot water. The rules allow you to roll over your gain from the sale of your house only once every two years—unless you take a new job in another location or are transferred as part of your old job.

What if your new home costs less than your old one?

This is the key question for retirees thinking of trading down. The answer? If you buy a new house or condominium and it costs less than the adjusted selling price of your old home, you must report on your Form 1040 the difference in price.

That is, you must report the difference between the adjusted selling price of your old house and the amount you paid for your new one.

Then, Uncle Sam says, you must pay taxes on that amount, although he allows you to defer the remainder of any gain you realize from the sale.

What if you're age 55 or older?

In this case, Uncle Sam gives you a break.

He allows you to sell your primary residence and pocket up to $125,00 of any profit free of taxes. (Any amount in excess of $125,000 is taxed as a capital gain.)

The $125,000 limit applies to a single person or a married couple filing jointly. What if you're married and file separately? The ceiling comes to $62,500 per spouse.

But the rules state that you're eligible for this tax break only if you're 55 years of age or older before the day you sell your home.

The rules treat a married couple filing jointly as one person. So you qualify for the tax break if either you or your spouse is age 55 before the sale, and you both are owners of the home.

Also, the rules say, you qualify for the exclusion only

if your home is your principal residence for at least three of the five years immediately prior to the sale.

However, the house doesn't have to be your principal residence at the time it's sold. Uncle Sam says that up to two years may pass between the time you vacate the house and the actual sale, as long as you lived in your home for the three years before you vacated it.

The rules also require you to notify the IRS that you're making use of the exclusion by filing Form 2119, "Sale or Exchange of Principal Residence," with your annual 1040.

TIP You should know that the $125,000 exclusion is a once-in-a-lifetime deal. Under the rules, you may exclude a profit on the sale of your home from your taxable income only if you didn't previously take advantage of this break.

What if you or your spouse remarry? Neither one of you may claim the $125,000 exclusion if either of you took it before.

TIP Plan carefully when it comes to this tax break. It's far too valuable to waste. Here's an example of how you could lose some of its benefits.

In early 1962, you purchased a house for what was then a hefty sum of $30,000. In 1991—shortly after you turn 55—you and your spouse decide to sell.

Your idea is to invest your tax-free profit in securities, then move to the oceanside Florida vacation cottage you bought some years ago.

You sell your old place for $130,000.

To calculate your profit, you subtract your houses's original cost—$30,000—and a 6 percent real estate agent's commission—$7,800.

The result is $92,200. When you file your joint return, you let the IRS know that you're taking advantage of the one-time, age-55, home-sale exclusion.

You invest your $92,200 in tax-free municipal bonds and move south. So far so good, but not so fast.

You used only $92,200 of the amount of gain that Uncle Sam permits you to exclude. And the difference, $32,800, between the amount you used and the amount the law allows—$125,000—is gone forever. The reason is simple. As we've seen, you can use this exclusion only once in your lifetime.

This provision is fine if you can exclude the maximum amount you're allowed or close to it. But you can't exclude the difference at some future date.

If you'd waited a year or two before you sold your home, you might have been better off. By then, the housing market might have improved, and you could have obtained a better price. Then you would have been able to take better advantage of this once-in-a-lifetime tax break.

TIP Here's some advice for people who own more than one home. It doesn't make sense to use the $125,000 exclusion now if you can make better use of it later.

Say you're moving for a year to your vacation home in upstate New York and you've just sold your old homestead.

Your vacation home has appreciated more in value than the house you just sold, so why not wait to claim the $125,000 exclusion until you sell your New York property?

That way, you can make better use of the exclusion.

Is there any way you can buy down without paying a capital gain tax?

You can make a really impressive tax-free maneuver by combining the $125,000 exclusion and the sale-and-replacement, or rollover, break.

By combining these two provisions in the tax code, you may collect more than $125,000 in profit and buy a much less expensive home without paying a single penny in taxes.

Here's an example of how this strategy can work.

Say you paid $165,000 for your house in 1974, then 17 years later you sell it for $380,000. You collect an impressive $215,000 profit. Since you are fifty-six years old, you sensibly opt to take the one-time exclusion. So $125,000 of your $215,000 gain is tax free to you—forever.

Now, you want to purchase a new house. You may think you have to find one of equal value to your old one, so you'll qualify for the sale-and-replacement break. But wait a minute.

When it comes time to figure out how much you must spend on a new home, the rules allow you to subtract the amount of your exclusion—$125,000—from the selling price of your old home—$380,000. So you must spend only $255,000 for a new house—not $380,000.

As long as your new principal residence costs $255,000 or more, you defer paying taxes on your remaining gain of $90,000. And you reduce the basis of your new house by only the $90,000 gain that you don't pay taxes on now.

Now that you know some of the tax issues you may face in retirement, let's address a subject that comes up increasingly frequently today: retiring early. Is it a good idea or not? In the next chapter, we'll find out.

28

Should You Retire Early?

These days, more and more companies are offering tempting sweeteners to encourage employees to retire early. Maybe your company is one of them.

What should you do if you're asked to retire early? One place to start is with this chapter. Here, we give you the information you require to take stock of an early retirement offer—or just to decide to retire at an age that's younger than average.

What's included in an early retirement offer?

Most early retirement offers provide employees with a host of benefits—from cash payments and an enhanced or sweetened pension to post-retirement medical policies and offers of outplacement counselling or help in finding a new job. Many companies provide early retirees with financial planning assistance to help them evaluate the offer.

Let's start with cash payments. In most cases, these are based on your wages and the number of years you worked for the company. For example, you might receive one month's salary for each year of service.

When it comes to calculating the pension you'll receive, many companies add extra years of service to determine your annual benefit. Say your company wants you to retire early. It says it will pay you an annual pension equal to your years of service times 1 percent. Then it multiplies the result times your average compensation during the three years when you earned the most money.

Say you worked for 20 years. Your early retirement package would give you another 5 years. So you'd multiply 25 years times 1 percent to get 25 percent of your average earnings, instead of 20 years times 1 percent.

Many companies also "adjust" your age when they figure your pension benefits for early retirement. Here's an example. Say you're 58 years old, and your company offers you early retirement. The fly in the ointment? Your company's pension plan doesn't allow workers to retire with full benefits until they reach age 62.

So to make retiring early more attractive to you, your employer adds five years to your age, which brings you

to 63, one year beyond the age your company requires for a full pension.

What would happen if your company doesn't add years to your age when it calculates your pension for early retirement? You'd still qualify for a pension, but you'd receive less than you would at the full pension age of 62.

Another element of an early retirement package can be free medical and reduced group life insurance coverage for one year—although, with rising medical insurance costs, this benefit is becoming increasingly scarce.

What do you do after the year is up? The law requires employers to allow you to pay for medical insurance coverage yourself at its group rate for an additional 6 months.

Many companies, though, do more than the law requires.

Often, you can continue your medical coverage as part of the group until you reach age sixty-five, when Medicare kicks in. At that point, your company health insurance may be canceled.

Other companies, however, allow you the option of signing up for a separate plan that supplements Medicare. In this case, Medicare, plus the separate plan, provide benefits that are the same as those you had enjoyed before age sixty-five.

Sound attractive to you?

For the most part, these early retirement packages are worthwhile, which explains why so many employees take advantage of them. But you should think through the offer carefully before you accept.

What's the first step in evaluating a retirement offer?

If you're like most people, one of the key reasons you want to hold onto your job is money. You're not sure if you can afford to quit.

There's an easy way to find out. You just calculate how much more you will earn working full-time rather than not working at all. We call this difference the *marginal value* of continuing to work; in other words, the difference that working makes in your income.

Probably, you'll take home more as a worker than as a retiree. The question is how much extra? The answer may surprise you. Take a look at the tables that follow. They show how much more income a hypothetical employee—we'll call her Molly—can earn by working full time.

In our tables, we assume that Molly is sixty-two years old and can collect Social Security benefits. We also calculate her federal income taxes using 1991 tax rates. We gave Molly two personal exemptions and used the standard deduction rather than itemizing deductions. Also, as you'll see, we figured in only federal taxes. State taxes could take another bite.

	Working	*Retired*
Salary	$42,000	-
Social Security	(3,213)	$ 9,380
Pension plan income	-	16,800
401(k) plan income	-	3,451
Federal income tax	(4,811)	(1,496)
Commuting expenses	(1,000)	-
Other work-related expenses (clothes, meals, dry cleaning, etc.)*	(2,100)	-
After-tax income	$30,876	$28,135
Marginal income	$2,741	
Marginal hourly income	1.40	

* These expenses are estimated at 5 percent of salary, a common rule of thumb.

Surprising as it may seem, Molly takes home only $2,741 more each year by continuing to work than she'd receive if she gave up her job. And the amount she earns each hour—based on a standard work year of 1,960 hours—adds up to only $1.40.

What Molly should ask herself is whether she needs to work full time all year round to take home a scant $2,741 after taxes. Maybe she can earn just as much by working part time—at a job with less work-related expense and less stress.

She'd still have the benefits of working—a stimulating environment, a sense of accomplishment, social interaction, sometimes even medical benefits—without giving up her other interests.

Let's consider another scenario with a higher salary. Again, we'll assume Molly is age sixty-two and can collect Social Security benefits. And we'll calculate her federal income taxes the same way we did in our previous example.

	Working	*Retired*
Salary	$75,000	-
Social Security	(3,924)	$ 9,400
Pension plan income	-	20,250
IRA income	-	13,750
401(k) income		1,850
Federal income tax	(16,908)	(7,464)
Commuting expenses	(1,000)	-
Other work-related expenses (clothes, meals, dry cleaning, etc.)*	(3,750)	-
After tax income	$59,418	$47,786
Marginal income	$11,632	
Marginal hourly income	$5.93	

* These expenses are estimated at 5 percent of salary, a common rule of thumb

Why not try your own analysis of your situation? You may be surprised at how affordable it would be for you to retire early. Just fill in the blanks on the following chart:

	Working	*Retired*
Salary	\$_____	\$_____
Social Security	_____	_____
Pension plan income	_____	_____
IRA income	_____	_____
401(k) income	_____	_____
Federal income tax	_____	_____
Commuting expenses	_____	_____
Other work-related expenses (clothes, meals, dry cleaning, etc.)*	_____	_____
After tax income	_____	_____
Marginal income	_____	_____
Marginal hourly income	_____	_____

* These expenses are estimated at 5 percent of salary, a common rule of thumb

What pension benefits will you receive?

If you're offered early retirement, you need to take a look at the pension benefits you'll receive. Will your benefits be cut because you're retiring early? Will you receive enough to fund your retirement adequately until you qualify for Social Security benefits? How do your early retirement benefits compare with those you'd

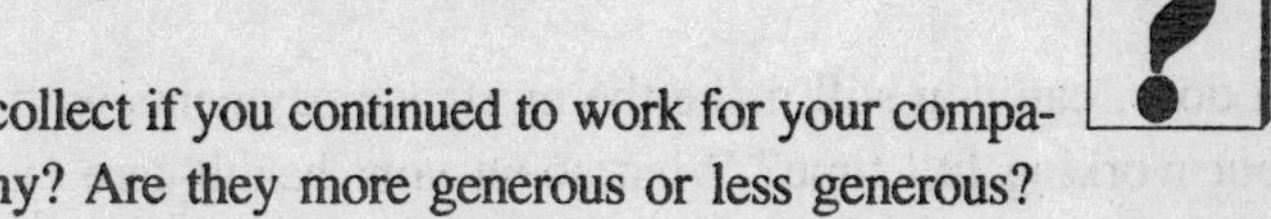

collect if you continued to work for your company? Are they more generous or less generous?

Say you hadn't planned to retire until five or even ten years from now. Your early-retirement benefits might be considerably less than those you'd anticipated receiving—or they might not. If they are, it may be necessary for you take on another job to make up for the difference.

What are your payout options and tax situation?

When you take early retirement, many companies say that you can receive your pension either as a lump sum or over time in the form of an annuity. See chapters 21 and 22 to understand the advantage of each option.

What is your cash flow?

We've provided a retirement cash-flow worksheet in the appendix. Turn to it now, and fill it out as if you've already decided to retire early.

And don't avoid the tough questions.

Does the bank still hold a mortgage on your house? If

it does, can you still make the mortgage payments without working full time? What about your health-care expenses? You'll need to pay for medical coverage, if it's not part of your early-retirement offer.

Also, do you anticipate income from other sources—an inheritance, perhaps, to up your income in your golden years.

With your answers to these questions—plus the cash-flow worksheet—you have a realistic idea of whether you can afford to opt for early retirement.

What are your options outside the company?

Some people have to—or want to—work after they retire. If you're one of them and you've been offered early retirement, think about your odds of finding another job. That's where a professional outplacement counselor comes in handy. If your employer doesn't provide this service, you may want to foot the bill yourself.

Should you seek advice from an outsider?

Deciding whether to accept an offer of early retirement is serious business. It never hurts to consult a professional. So we suggest that you consult with an accountant or financial planner before acting on an early retirement offer.

29

Mastering the Fundamentals

Planning an estate involves both financial and nonfinancial objectives. On the financial side, you want to minimize or eliminate such expenses as taxes that are associated with transferring assets at your death. And the nonfinancial goals? Most people want to make sure they provide properly for those who are financially dependent on them and leave something to people—or organizations—about whom they care.

Estate planning can be difficult—not only because of the financial complexities, but because the process brings you face to face with your own mortality. Moreover, estate planning is a big responsibility as you try to foresee the time when you'll no longer be around to make decisions. Other people—particularly people you love—will be affected by the plans you make now, and they'll be expected to exercise their own judgment once you're gone.

In this chapter, we'll take a look at one of the more difficult steps in estate planning—deciding not only who gets what but when. We'll also discuss the important issue of life insurance. Finally, we'll provide information that's critical for surviving spouses.

Let's start, though, with a quick word to the wise. The best time to start your estate planning is now. The longer you wait to begin, the better the chance that your heirs will be left to shoulder your responsibilities.

Who will be your beneficiaries?

This decision is, of course, very personal. Most people want to plan for their spouse, a significant other, children, and close relatives first. They might also want to leave a legacy to their alma mater or to a favorite charity.

Keep in mind, however, that practicality alone doesn't dictate what you leave and to whom. Your personal philosophy also plays a part and affects what you do with your money while you're alive.

For instance, you may consider it your responsibility to leave a legacy for your children. Or you may think, as some people do, that your only responsibility to your offspring is to provide them with as good an education as you can. In this case, you may decide to dispose of much of your estate while you're still living.

How much will you leave your children?

"That's easy," you may first think. 'After my spouse and I are gone, our children will share equally in our estate." Before you come to this conclusion, however, it may be a good idea to ponder the matter more deeply.

You need to consider what effect large bequests might have on your children. Will they use their inheritance wisely? Might inheriting a tidy sum stifle their ambition?

What about a family business? Do your children want to run the business and have they the skills and talent to do so? Or are you trying to live your dreams through them?

In the case of a family business, the best idea is to ask your children what they would like. In fact, that's a good idea, period.

When your children are old enough, discuss with them the general size of your estate and what you plan to do with it. That way, they'll know exactly what to expect, and you'll have a chance to listen to their views.

It also makes sense to observe how your children have handled money over the years. Are they responsible with an allowance, say? Have they earned money on their own? What have they done with their earnings?

Maybe you think your children won't be mature enough to handle a sudden financial windfall. Many parents don't, and their solution is to tie up the money they leave as long as they think is necessary.

Though eighteen or twenty-one is considered the legal coming of age in most states, you can state in your will that your children can't collect their inheritance until they reach thirty, say, or thirty-five. Or you can structure a trust that gives them access to interest, but prevents them from touching principal.

Some people design trusts that don't pay out until the child gets his or her college degree or shows proof of earning a salary.

Also, you may provide an inheritance for your children, but not for your grandchildren. That way, your children can decide what will be good for their offspring decades from now.

Do you need life insurance?

Your need for life insurance changes as you grow older. Sometimes you need sizeable amounts of coverage, and sometimes you don't.

Most people, if they work for someone else, receive

ABC

life insurance from their employers. When they retire, however, their coverage ends or is considerably reduced. If you want additional coverage—or coverage at all—you have to buy your own policy. So you need to rethink your life insurance needs when you retire.

When do you need life insurance? There are five situations when you might want to have it.

First, say you have a pension, which will be reduced when you die. In this case, your spouse will have less to live on than he or she has now. In addition, your Social Security benefit will be less after your death. So you probably want to buy enough life insurance to make up the amount your spouse will lose.

Second, you may need life insurance to cover your final expenses—medical bills, the cost of your funeral, and so on. You may want to look into a so-called burial policy that will cover the amount you need for these purposes.

What's the third instance in which you need life insurance? To provide your estate with liquidity. Say, for instance, you own a business, which is your primary asset. Since you want your family to keep the business after you die, you need the proceeds from a life insurance policy to pay the estate taxes.

Or say that most of your assets are tied up in real estate. Again, your survivors would use the proceeds from a life insurance policy to pay the estate taxes on your real estate holdings, which they don't want to sell.

Fourth, you may want to leave your spouse or children with a sizeable estate, one that's larger than you've been able to amass in your lifetime. In this case, you can use the proceeds from a life insurance policy to make a "final gift" to your loved ones.

Finally, you may want to purchase a life insurance policy to pay off what you owe—the mortgage on the family home, say—when you die. That way, your survivors aren't burdened with debt after your death.

If you do need—or want—to buy life insurance, what type of policy is right for you? You should know that life insurance comes in two general forms: term and whole life.

With term insurance, you pay for only the so-called death benefit—the amount your beneficiaries receive when you die. Whole life, by contrast, has an investment component. Part of your premium pays for the insurance portion of the policy; part the insurance company invests on your behalf.

Term insurance is less expensive at first, since you're buying *only* insurance. However, it does become increasingly expensive as you grow older. A whole life policy, by contrast, will cost considerably more than term, but has the advantage of a fixed premium. You

pay the same amount each year regardless of your health or age.

The bottom line, then, is to shop around and compare before purchasing a life insurance policy.

Now, on to the financial aspects of estate planning.

...ay the same amount each year regardless of
...ou reach 70 or so.

The bottom line, then, is to shop around and compare before purchasing a life insurance policy.

Now, on to the financial aspect of estate planning.

1251 Avenue of the Americas
New York, NY 10020

Telephone 212 489 8900

Price Waterhouse

October 1990

Dear Clients and Friends of Price Waterhouse:

Price Waterhouse is pleased to present you with the enclosed set of comprehensive personal financial planning books:

- **The Price Waterhouse Investors' Tax Adviser**
- **The Price Waterhouse Personal Tax Adviser**
- **The Price Waterhouse Retirement Planning Adviser**

These books address the impact of taxes on your day-to-day finances and investments as well as the consequences of financial and other issues on retirement. The information they provide will [illegible] informed choices when working

Peter J. Hart
Vice Chairman--Tax
Price Waterhouse

30

Making Sense of Estate Taxes

We've now taken a look at the nonfinancial aspects of estate planning, so let's move on to the financial considerations—starting with estate taxes.

How much of your estate is subject to tax?

Say your total estate is worth $600,000 or less. In this case, none of it is subject to federal tax. However, be forewarned: It's easy to underestimate by a considerable amount an estate's size. And, if you do, you might find yourself saddled with an estate tax bill that you didn't anticipate.

Of course, what you really need to know isn't the gross value of your estate but the amount that Uncle Sam will tax—in other words, your taxable estate. So the first thing you should do is figure out this taxable value. Doing so isn't difficult.

Just add up your cash on hand and your other assets—certificates of deposit, bonds, stocks, mutual funds, real estate, the face value of your life insurance, and so on.

You'll also need to account for not-so-obvious assets, such as the amounts that have been adding up as part of your compensation and fringe benefit packages.

You should also add in the value of personal property—automobiles, antiques, jewelry, and so forth, and your half of any property held jointly.

The next step in estimating your taxable estate is to subtract your liabilities, such as a mortgage, the amount you'll spend on funeral and burial expenses (figure $3,000 to $5,000), and the estimated costs of administering your estate (you should estimate 2 to 5 percent of the estate's gross value). You should also subtract any charitable bequests that you've made in your will.

Are there any tax breaks you need to know about?

Indeed there are—the unlimited marital deduction and the unified credit. The unlimited marital deduction, as its name implies, lets you bequeath free of tax your full estate—whether it adds up to $1,000, $100,000, $1 million or more—to your spouse. Uncle Sam does get his due eventually, but not until your spouse dies.

Say you die and leave your husband $2 million. That amount passes to him free of tax. Two years after your death, your spouse remarries. He, of course, also can use the marital deduction when it comes to the estate he will bequeath. When he dies, he can leave everything to his new wife tax free. Or, if the wife dies first, she can leave her assets tax free to him.

Sooner or later your estate and any additions that have been made to it will go to someone who is not a surviving spouse—a child, for example, or a relative. When that day comes, the benefit of the marital deduction ends, and Uncle Sam collects his due.

What happens if you don't leave your entire estate to your spouse? In this case, you subtract the portion bequeathed to your spouse from your total estate. The remainder is your taxable estate and subject to estate taxes. However, as we explain below, all or a portion of this amount may not be taxed, thanks to the unified credit.

What is the unified tax credit?

It is an exemption from taxation for estates that add up to $600,000 or less. Anyone can use the credit, not just married couples. It works like this:

Say you die in 1990. You never married, have no

children, and decide to bequeath your total estate of $600,000 to your beloved younger brother. Your brother is also the executor of your estate, so he files Form 706, the estate tax return with Uncle Sam within nine months of your death, as the law requires.

You should know that a separate tax schedule—which you'll find printed below—applies to estates. (This is exactly the same schedule that applies to gifts.) As the value of your estate increases, so do the tax rates. Your brother looks at the schedule and computes an estate tax of $192,800. Next, he subtracts from that tax the amount of the unified credit, which is also $192,800.

The result, of course, is zero, which means Uncle Sam collects no taxes from your estate.

Say, though, you bequeath an estate that adds up to more than $600,000? Estate taxes add up quickly. If, you had left your brother $700,000 instead of $600,000, Uncle Sam would have collected $37,000 or 37 percent of the $100,000 that topped $600,000.

ESTATE AND GIFT TAXES

If Your Taxable Estate Is Between		You Owe	Plus %	On Amount Over
$ - -	$ 10,000	$ -	18%	$ -
10,000	20,000	1,800	20	10,000
20,000	40,000	3,800	22	20,000
40,000	60,000	8,200	24	40,000
60,000	80,000	13,000	26	60,000
80,000	100,000	18,200	28	80,000
100,000	150,000	23,800	30	100,000
150,000	250,000	38,800	32	150,000
250,000	500,000	70,800	34	250,000
500,000	750,000	155,800	37	500,000
750,000	1,000,000	248,300	39	750,000
1,000,000	1,250,000	345,800	41	1,000,000
1,250,000	1,500,000	448,300	43	1,250,000
1,500,000	2,000,000	555,800	45	1,500,000
2,000,000	2,500,000	780,800	49	2,000,000
2,500,000	3,000,000	1,025,800	53	2,500,000
3,000,000	10,000,000	1,290,800	55	3,000,000
10,000,000	21,040,000	5,140,800	60	10,000,000
21,040,000		11,764,800	55	21,040,000

What strategies can you use to reduce estate taxes?

Your first tack should be to try to maximize your use of the unified credit. How? As we saw, the rules let you bequeath your assets to your spouse tax-free. However, it's not always a good idea to do so.

Here's an example. Say Mitch dies in 1991 and leaves an estate worth $1.2 million to his wife Barbara. Thanks to the marital deduction, no federal taxes are due on this amount. Barbara dies four years later and bequeaths the estate to the couple's two children.

We'll assume the estate hasn't grown and still comes to $1.2 million. The unified credit shelters only $600,000 from federal taxation. So the estate must pony up a hefty tax of $235,000 on the remaining $600,000.

Here's an idea that will work better. Mitch shouldn't leave the entire $1.2 million to Barbara. Instead, he should divide the amount into two shares. He leaves the marital portion to Barbara. But the unified credit shelter share—what's known in estate-planning jargon as the *bypass share*—goes to the two children after Barbara dies.

Mitch puts the bypass share in a trust—known, appropriately enough, as a *bypass* or *credit shelter trust*. Barbara receives income from this trust as long as she lives. When she dies, the principal goes to the couple's two children.

This strategy has two advantages: Mitch and Barbara don't squander the tax benefit of the unified credit—and, more important, they save a tidy $235,000 in estate taxes. That's because Mitch left part of the estate to Barbara, and that amount escapes taxation thanks to the marital deduction. The remaining $600,000 is in trust for Barbara and the kids—and that amount isn't taxed because of the unified credit. When Barbara dies, her

TAX

estate adds up to only $600,000, the amount actually received from Mitch and not put in the trust, and, again, the unified credit keeps that sum out of Uncle Sam's pocket. You should know that these trusts can be funded only with assets that pass through your will. Property held jointly, life insurance proceeds, and retirement assets typically pass by title or contract and override any provisions in your will.

A second idea: Set up a Q-TIP trust. What is a Q-TIP? The law contains a provision for something known as the *qualified terminable interest property.*

A Q-TIP is not so much a tax-saving device as a device that both lets you take advantage of the unlimited marital deduction and lets you decide who gets these assets after your spouse dies. In other words, a Q-TIP gives you the ability to maintain control of your assets long after you're dead and buried.

Here's an example. Say you state in your will that your wife should receive all your stock holdings.

The result: Your wife receives annual income from the stock—but only for her lifetime. Additionally, she may be able to sell the stock and use the funds, but only for her own use. The stock goes to your daughter after your wife passes away. Since the bequest qualifies for the estate tax marital deduction, the estate pays no taxes until your wife dies.

Using a Q-TIP is especially effective if you've had a previous marriage. The reason? It lets you ensure that the beneficiaries of your choice, your children, for example, will eventually inherit your estate. At the same time, however, it allows you to grant your second spouse a life estate in your property.

You may have noticed that the Q-TIP trust and the bypass trust are quite similar. With both, the spouse receives income from the trust, while the rest goes to your children when your spouse dies. The major difference is how much control your spouse has over the principal. Another key difference is the fact that an election that is made with the estate tax return allows the Q-TIP to qualify for the marital deduction.

Are there other strategies you can use?

Making gifts to slash the size of your estate often makes sense. As you probably know, each year you may give up to $10,000 free of gift tax to each of your children—or to anyone else of your choosing.

Say your spouse gives as well. In this case, you may both bequeath up to $20,000 annually to each recipient. So if you are married and have two children, you and

TAX

your spouse may give away tax free up to $40,000; if you have four children, you could give away $80,000 annually, and so forth.

While giving gifts makes for good tax planning, you should make sure you can afford to do so. If you can, you'll find that giving away your assets while you're still alive can save you an impressive amount in estate tax. How? Here's an example.

Say the total of your taxable estate is $2.4 million. You know that if you wait until you die to distribute the money, your heirs will get stuck with a huge estate tax bill.

The solution? Both you and your spouse begin to give $20,000 to each of your three children every year. They have no objection, and, by the end of ten years, you've given away $600,000, with no tax consequences whatsoever.

The result: You've saved for your heirs a whopping $286,000 in estate tax. (This calculation assumes that the $600,000 wouldn't have increased in value and that you would have spent, not saved, any earnings on the principal.)

Now, you've accomplished two important goals: You've divvied up some of your assets among those dearest to you— and you've slashed your estate tax bill.

What happens if you give someone more than the $10,000 annual limit, or $20,000 for a married couple?

If you give amounts that top the $10,000 annual exclusion, you use up your lifetime unified credit. This provision in the law means you can give amounts of up to $600,000 ($1,200,000 for a married couple) more than the annual exclusion before you'll fork over a gift tax. Note, too, that you pay the gift tax, not the recipient.

Is giving over the limit a good idea? It is if you feel comfortable financially and want to be exceptionally generous to your family while you're still alive. It's also a good idea if you want to get appreciating assets out of your estate.

What about gifts to charities?

Naturally, if you make charitable contributions while you're living, they are no longer part of your estate, since what you gave away is no longer yours.

But what about those charitable bequests in your will? The good news? Your estate can deduct these gifts for estate tax purposes. So be as generous as you like with your charitable contributions.

What about life insurance proceeds?

Here's one idea: You can remove the proceeds of any life insurance from the estate. That way, these proceeds aren't added to your estate's value. There's a hitch though. To remove life insurance from an estate means you must give up all ownership privileges to the policy. You can relinquish your ownership in two ways: Either you can transfer the policy directly to a beneficiary or you can set up an irrevocable life insurance trust.

Like the bypass trust, this type of trust can provide income to your surviving spouse during his or her lifetime and pass the remaining value of your estate to your beneficiaries when your spouse dies.

There's one pitfall you must avoid when it comes to transferring policies. For an existing policy, you must transfer the policy more than three years before your death. Otherwise, the law treats the transfer as if it never occurred, and the proceeds are automatically included in the value of your estate. However, a life insurance trust can acquire a new policy at any time.

What if the combined estate of you and your spouse comes to less than $600,000?

As far as federal taxes go, planning for this size estate is easy. You have no taxes to worry about thanks to the marital deduction and the unified credit. What you may have to concern yourself with, though, are state and local taxes. So try to structure your assets to avoid these taxes. Since, too, you most likely want to provide for any children, you and your spouse might write wills bequeathing your estate to the surviving spouse—or to your children if only one spouse is alive.

What if your combined estate is between $600,000 and $1.2 million?

This size estate can be quite difficult to plan. Here's why: You can often set in motion a strategy that may help you when it comes to taxes, but really isn't too practical. Here's an example.

Say you want to avoid estate taxes entirely, so you arrange that each of you have no more than $600,000 in assets while you both are alive. After you die, say, you've arranged that your spouse not be left with more than $600,000.

Here are the problems with this idea. From a practical point of view, the spouse who has more money usually hasn't enough in liquid assets to transfer funds to the spouse with less money. Moreover, the survivor, especially if he or she is young, might well feel more comfortable with access to more than $600,000.

So what can you do if your estate is of this intermediate size? The first thing you should do is transfer enough liquid assets to bring the "poorer" spouse's wealth up to $600,000. Do so within the bounds of common sense, however. And keep in mind that you're relinquishing control over these assets.

Then, each spouse should leave his or her entire estate to the other spouse. But each spouse should also have the ability to "disclaim assets"—that is, choose not to inherit them. If he or she does disclaim them, they pass to a bypass trust.

If you take these steps, you'll have some flexibility, if an estate tax problem crops up for the surviving spouse. In fact, as a surviving spouse you have three choices. You can remove the assets from the estate by disclaiming them and placing them in the credit shelter trust; you can simply spend the money, or you can make tax-free gifts to members of your family, friends, or a favorite charity to reduce the estate.

What if your combined estate tops $1.2 million?

When an estate tops $1.2 million, you'll find that the appreciation of your remaining assets usually offsets gifts you've made to family members.

Say, then, your estate comes to more than $1.2 million. In this case, you may want to limit your gift giving to meet specific needs—a down payment on a house, for instance—rather than setting up a regular gift-giving program.

Also, you and your spouse's wills should contain credit shelter trusts with the balance going to the surviving spouse, either outright, in a "regular" marital trust, or in a Q-TIP trust.

Here's another idea to consider—"second-to-die" life insurance policies. These policies pay off after your surviving spouse dies. Since assets from the first death can pass free of tax utilizing the marital deduction, the payment of tax doesn't usually occur until the surviving spouse dies. Because the policy is insuring joint lives, more premiums will be paid over a longer time period than under a conventional single life policy. Because of this, the annual premiums on these policies are normally significantly lower.

There's one last—and critical—item you need to know about when you're planning your estate: how to write your will. That's the subject of our next chapter.

31

Getting the Will That You Need

People who fail to make wills don't suffer; their heirs do. In fact, those whom you love the most may inherit the least—or nothing at all.

So if you're one of the six out of ten Americans who don't have a will, we hope that you'll make one. And if you have made a will, we hope that you'll look it over periodically. In this chapter, we'll tell you what you need to know about wills.

What if you die without a will?

If you die without having made a will, you've died "intestate." What that means is that a court in your home state will select someone—in most cases, your surviving spouse—to take charge of your estate.

What's wrong with that arrangement? Well, maybe nothing. On the other hand, it could be fraught with problems.

Say, for instance, this is your second marriage and you have children from both marriages? Are you sure that your present spouse will treat the children from both marriages evenhandedly? You can't count on it.

Or say just your children survive you? Many state courts give each child an equal voice in the administration of a parent's estate. That type of arrangement, again, may be fine. Or it could lead to messy arguments about who will inherit what.

Even if you don't face any of these problems, not having a will could prove expensive. Many state courts require estate administrators to post a bond of $1,000 or more. That money will come from the assets of your estate.

Do you need an attorney to prepare your will?

We'll get to this question in a minute, but first a few basics.

You should know that the two chief types of wills are *witnessed wills* and *holographic* or *handwritten* wills. All states recognize the validity of witnessed wills, but only a handful—Arkansas, California, Iowa, Kentucky,

Louisiana, Mississippi, Montana, Nevada, North Carolina, North Dakota, South Dakota, Tennessee, Texas, Utah, Virginia, West Virginia, and Wyoming—recognize holographic wills.

Even in those seventeen states, holographic wills must be written, dated, and signed in your hand and have no other printed or typed material on them, if they're to be declared valid. If you have a witnessed will, it doesn't matter if it's typed or handwritten. However, it's only valid and legal if witnesses have signed it.

So you could write out or type your will, have two or three people—neither of whom are public notaries—witness it, and feel reasonably confident that the document would stand up against any court challenges.

We say two or three witnesses, because the number required varies depending on the state where you live. Most states require that you have at least two witnesses to your signature. But seven states—Connecticut, Georgia, Maine, New Hampshire, South Carolina, and Vermont—require that three people witness the signing of a will.

You've probably heard of a do-it-yourself witnessed will, called a statutory will. This is simply a printed form that comes with written instructions for filling in the blanks. Sometimes stationery stores sell these wills or you can obtain them from your local bar association.

Many states accept them as valid, but that doesn't mean you should use them.

They may be fine if your estate is quite modest and your bequests entirely straightforward, but we recommend that you take no chances. And that brings us back to our original question—should you hire an attorney to prepare your will? We think you should—it's worth the modest cost. With an attorney preparing your will, you can be confident that your last testament is valid and contains the necessary clauses and provisions to accomplish your goals.

What does a will contain?

You're the so-called testator, and the first paragraph of a will states your name and address. It also says that you're making your will knowingly and revoking all previous wills.

Following this information comes a statement that tells your *executor*—who is the person or persons you name to administer your estate and make sure your assets get distributed as you wish—to pay all your debts, taxes, and burial expenses promptly. These three items are the first claims against your estate.

You should know that unless you explicitly state otherwise, each gift you bequeath in your will may bear a pro rata portion of the debts, expenses, and taxes in your estate—even a favorite bowl you left to Aunt Sally. That means if you want these expenses paid from some other pool of assets, you should say so explicitly.

Naturally, the main reason you're writing your will is to mandate those whom you want to receive your assets after you're gone. And that's what most of your will is about.

Listed in your will first are so-called specific bequests. What's a specific bequest?

Say you want to leave a friend an heirloom watch or some other personal property, $25,000 in municipal bonds, for example. Or say you want to give a gift of cash or property to your favorite charity or to your alma mater. These gifts of personal property are known as specific bequests.

What do you need to know about specific bequests?

The rule about specific bequests: If you want to make sure an item with sentimental value—a special necklace, perhaps, or your childhood stamp collection—goes to a specific individual, make that wish perfectly clear in your will. If you don't, your executor will decide how these assets are divided.

Here's an idea. You may want to bequeath these items of sentimental value to one person you trust—your spouse, perhaps. Then you could list in a separate letter instructions on whom you want to receive these items. This type of letter is nonbinding, but that should be no problem as long as you choose someone on whom you can rely to distribute the gifts as you wish.

Why not just bequeath these items in your will? The problem with this strategy is you'll probably change your mind somewhere along the way. And, each time you do, you'll have to alter your will. That can get pricey. If you use our suggestion, you can change your nonbinding instructions as often as you like without changing your will.

Of course if you want to be 100 percent positive that a specific item goes to a specific person, you'll have to include that bequest in your will.

Next in your will come general bequests.

What is a general bequest?

Here's an example. Say you want to leave $5,000 to your first cousin, Joe Jones. So you say in your will—"I leave $5,000 to my first cousin, Joe Jones." Is that a specific or general bequest? You may think it's a specific bequest, but it's not.

Here's the way a specific bequest would be worded: "I leave to my first cousin, Joe Jones, the $5,000 I have in my money-market fund, Number 01604444, at the ABC Financial Institution."

A general bequest, then, doesn't specify from what specific source of funds it comes.

What is a residual estate?

It's what's left of your assets after you subtract all specific and general bequests.

Again, an example may help. Say you tell your executor to make three general gifts—$10,000 to each of your sisters, for example. You ask that all remaining assets be split equally among your surviving spouse and your children. Your residual estate are these remaining assets.

Recipients of specific and general bequests have first claim on your estate and, as we saw, specific legacies are paid before general legacies. That means you need to be careful. Make sure you have enough remaining in your estate for your principal beneficiaries after all debts, expenses, and taxes and your specific and general bequests are paid.

Here's another point to keep in mind: Consider what

would happen if your financial fortunes spiralled downward, and you didn't change your will? Would your residual estate—that part of your estate that goes to your primary heirs—be less than you had wished?

If you think it may be, you should review your specific and general bequests. You may want to do away with some of these.

Whom should you name as executor?

Next to naming a guardian, which we'll discuss next, this is probably the most significant decision you'll make. Why?

The executor is in charge of taking care of your estate until your assets are distributed. He or she is responsible for such tasks as filing your estate tax return and, perhaps, making investment decisions. For these reasons, it makes sense for the executor to have some knowledge about taxes and investments.

Your executor is entitled to a fee or commission, which is determined by the laws in each state. Some states let the courts determine these fees, while others base them on the size or complexity of your estate. As a rule, these fees come to about 1 to 3 percent of your gross estate.

Should you name two people to act as coexecutors,

the fees may double. So it's a good idea to ask your lawyer about the rules in your state before you name more than one executor.

Who do most people choose as their executor? Most name their spouse. Other popular choices include a trusted relative, friend, or business colleague.

If your estate is simple—a home, some cash and a little stock and insurance, say—it should take less than a year to settle, and your executor will probably encounter few difficulties. So there should be no problem choosing an unsophisticated family member or friend as executor. He or she can probably manage quite well with help from your attorney or accountant.

Say though you think there may be family arguments over your wishes. In these cases, it makes sense to name your attorney or some other adviser you trust as coexecutor. Moreover, if your estate is large and complex, you should name a professional—a trust company officer or a bank—to act as executor. Then you can add a trusted family member or friend as coexecutor.

It's general practice in writing wills to list a first, second, and third choice for executors. The third choice is usually an institution, such as a bank or trust company. The reason? You choose a third option just in case your first two choices aren't able fo fulfill these responsibilities.

What do you need to know about naming a guardian?

If you're the parent of a minor child or children, it's critical to name a guardian for these minors. You should know, though, that if you're divorced, the courts won't honor your choice of guardian as long as you are survived by a spouse who is the natural parent. That rule holds true even if you have full custody. If you die, your child automatically goes to your former spouse. However, say that your spouse predeceases you. In this case, you can make sure that your children have the guardian of your choice—not the court's—by naming that person in your will.

Here's another sound reason for naming a guardian: Doing so guarantees that your children would have a guardian of your choosing if you and your spouse both died simultaneously, in the same accident, for example. It's important, of course, to thoroughly talk over the matter with potential guardians before you finally settle on one. You want someone who is not only able to handle this important responsibility—but thoroughly willing.

If you're unable to decide on a guardian, you may want to designate someone in your will—your executor, perhaps—to name a guardian.

Should your will include anything else?

It should include any special instructions. For example, you may want to tell your executor to ask your heirs to carry on your business. Remember: If your will doesn't state what you want, your executors must do what they think is best. They are also bound by state laws, which may not give them the flexibility to handle your property as you intended.

It's also a good idea to state in a letter of instructions the kind of funeral you want or whether or not you want to be cremated. The more specific you can be, the less your family will have to worry about making these difficult decisions at an emotional time. Even more important, you can be reasonably sure that you get what you want.

What is a living will?

This is another document you might want to consider. A so-called living will states that you don't want to be kept alive by "heroic" or "extraordinary" means—life-support machines, for example. These documents aren't legally binding in some states. Nonetheless, you will have formally let your family and friends know how you feel about these heroic measures.

What will your attorney need to know?

To draw up your will, your attorney needs to know your full legal name, date of birth, Social Security number, address, and telephone number. So type out this information, and bring it to your lawyer at your first visit. He or she also needs this same information for your beneficiaries. You should include, too, full legal names and addresses for any charities or institutions you plan to mention in your will.

Your attorney also will ask about your marital history. Are you currently married? Were you ever divorced? If you were, what are the names of your former spouses? Does your divorce decree require that you bequeath certain assets to your former spouse or to your children? Your attorney will want to make sure that former spouses exercise no claim on your estate—unless you want them to.

Also, keep in mind that it is you, not your attorney, who, in the last analysis, must make sure that your will precisely expresses your intent. You want your will to be clear enough so that your heirs—or any court, for that matter—can determine your desires.

How long does a will remain valid?

Your will remains valid unless it's revoked. That means your will should change if your circumstances do. The law assumes that the last will you made accurately expresses what you want, even if that document is forty or fifty years old.

Is there anything you can't bequeath in your will?

Though it may seem strange, there are some possessions that the law says you can't dispose of through a will. For example, death benefits paid by a life insurance company usually go directly to a beneficiary named in the policy. You don't bequeath them in your will.

Property held in joint tenancy—for instance, your home or bank accounts—may also not be willed. If you and your spouse own your house as joint tenants, say, the spouse who survives automatically takes title of the property when the other dies. However, unfair as it may seem, the value of this property is still added to your gross estate for tax purposes.

Also, pension benefits for which you have named a

beneficiary don't go through your will. Neither do U.S. savings bonds if you've named a beneficiary in case of your death.

Where should you keep your will?

Your executor should know where you keep your will, so he or she can get to it. Never store your will where it could get stolen, destroyed, forgotten, mislaid, or lost.

One idea is to leave a photocopy in your bank safe deposit box, then ask your lawyer or accountant to put the original in his or her safe.

Alternatively, if you name a bank or trust company as executor, ask a bank or trust officer to keep your will in the institution's vault. Then, leave a copy of your will at home—in a desk drawer, say, or filing cabinet. Finally, make sure you let your main beneficiaries know where you keep your will.

Epilogue

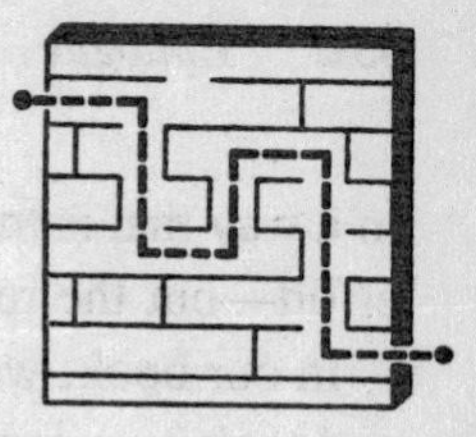

If you take away only one lesson from this book, make it this one: You and only you can make your retirement a satisfying one. Planning for your needs—be they financial, psychological or physiological—rests solely in your hands. No company, no government, no society will do it for you.

Retirement planning is, in reality, life planning. That thought underlies our whole approach to the retirement planning process. In fact, we look at retirement planning as not only a way to think about money but a way to think about yourself.

As you've seen, our approach to financial planning is built on answers to three simple questions: What do you have? What do you want? How do you get what you want?

We believe that if you answer these questions in as much detail as possible, you'll create a workable and successful plan for your retirement. Repeat the exercise every year or so or when your personal circumstances change, and you'll update your retirement plan.

The job isn't an easy one. To answer these questions

in a way that is truly helpful to you requires considerable effort—but the results are worth it.

In our book, we've provided you with the information and tools you need to answer these key questions. In the last analysis, though, no book can do your retirement planning for you. What we can do, however, is give you the means for developing your own retirement plan.

Remember, how well you live in retirement depends largely on what you do to prepare for it and the earlier the better. It is time now for you to get on with the process—time to resolve goals, complete your analysis and, even more important, to make decisions and take action.

Appendices

APPENDIX I

RETIREMENT SPENDING PLAN

Expense Category	*Currently*	↓—↑	*Retirement*
Housing	$______		$______
Utilities	______		______
Automobile	______		______
Life, Health Insurance	______		______
Food/Clothing/Grooming	______		______
Travel and Entertainment	______		______
Family Gifts	______		______
Charitable Gifts	______		______
Loan Repayments	______		______
Income Taxes	______		______
Social Security Taxes	______		______
Other/Including Savings	______		______
Total	$______		$______

APPENDIX IA

RETIREMENT SPENDING PLAN

Expense Category	*Currently*	↓—↑	*Retirement*
Housing	$14,200		$_____
Utilities	7,400		_____
Automobile	7,900		_____
Life, Health Insurance	3,900		_____
Food/Clothing/Grooming	8,000		_____
Travel and Entertainment	4,700		_____
Family Gifts	2,400		_____
Charitable Gifts	2,400		_____
Loan Repayments	2,400		_____
Income Taxes	14,200		_____
Social Security Taxes	5,200		_____
Other/Including Savings	17,300		_____
Total	$90,000		$63,000

APPENDIX II

Worksheet to Estimate Retirement Needs

Annual Retirement Income Goal (in Today's Dollars) (See Appendix I)	(A)	$_____
Estimated Social Security Benefits (See Appendix III)	(B)	(_____)
Pension Income	(C)	(_____)
Income Needed from Assets in Today's Dollars (A) − (B) − (C)	(D)	$_____
Income Needed from Assets At Retirement (adjusted for Inflation) (D) × Factor 1 (Appendix IV)	(E)	$_____
Capital Needed to Fund Income for Retirement Period (E) × Factor 2 (Appendix V)	(F)	$_____
Additional Capital Needed to Maintain Purchasing Power of Pension if not Adjusted for Inflation:		
Value of Pension at Retirement (C) × Factor 1 (Appendix IV)	(G)	$_____

Capital Needed to Maintain Purchasing Power of Pension (G) × Factor 3 (Appendix V)	(H)	______
Total Capital Required at Beginning of Retirement (F) + (H)	(I)	$______
Current Assets that are Available to fund Retirement (current value of. 401(k)s, IRAs, Profit Sharing Plans, and personal investments) (see Net Worth Statement in Appendix VIII)	(J)	$______
Value of those assets at Retirement (J) × Factor 4 (Appendix VI)	(K)	______
Additional Capital Required at Retirement (I) − (K)	(L)	$______

If this number is negative, stop here—you do not have to save additional amounts for retirement.

Amount to be saved each year to meet retirement goal (L) × Factor 5 (Appendix VII)	(M)	$______

APPENDIX III

Social Security Estimated Annual Benefit at Normal Retirement Age

Age in 1990	Annual Earnings $15,000	$20,000	$30,000	$40,000	$51,300	
65	$5,600	$6,600	$8,800	$10,700	$11,800	You
	2,800	3,300	4,400	5,300	5,900	Spouse
	8,400	9,900	13,200	16,000	17,700	Total
62	5,400	6,400	8,400	10,500	11,600	You
	2,700	3,200	4,200	5,200	5,800	Spouse
	8,100	9,600	12,600	15,700	17,400	Total
60	5,800	7,000	9,200	11,100	12,300	You
	2,900	3,500	4,600	5,500	6,100	Spouse
	8,700	10,500	13,800	16,600	18,400	Total
55	6,200	7,500	10,000	11,500	12,900	You
	3,100	3,700	5,000	5,700	6,400	Spouse
	9,300	11,200	15,000	17,200	19,300	Total
50	6,600	7,900	10,700	12,000	13,400	You
	3,300	3,900	5,300	6,000	6,700	Spouse
	9,900	11,800	16,000	18,000	20,100	Total
45	6,900	8,400	11,000	12,400	14,000	You
	3,400	4,200	5,500	6,200	7,000	Spouse
	10,300	12,600	16,500	18,600	21,000	Total
40	7,100	8,700	11,200	12,600	14,300	You
	3,500	4,300	5,600	6,300	7,100	Spouse
	10,600	13,000	16,800	18,900	21,400	Total
35	7,200	8,800	11,300	12,800	14,400	You
	3,600	4,400	5,600	6,300	7,200	Spouse
	10,800	13,200	16,900	19,100	21,600	Total

APPENDIX III

Social Security Estimated Annual Benefit at Early Retirement Age (62)

Age in 1990	Annual Earnings: $15,000	$20,000	$30,000	$40,000	$51,300	
62	$4,200	$4,900	$6,400	$7,900	$9,000	You
	1,900	2,300	3,000	3,700	4,200	Spouse
	6,100	7,200	9,400	11,600	13,200	Total
60	4,500	5,300	7,000	8,600	9,500	You
	2,100	2,500	3,300	4,000	4,400	Spouse
	6,600	7,800	10,300	12,600	13,900	Total
55	4,800	5,700	7,700	9,000	10,000	You
	2,200	2,700	3,600	4,200	4,700	Spouse
	7,000	8,400	11,300	13,200	14,700	Total
50	4,900	5,900	7,900	9,100	10,100	You
	2,200	2,600	3,600	4,100	4,500	Spouse
	7,100	8,500	11,500	13,200	14,600	Total
45	5,000	6,100	8,100	9,100	10,200	You
	2,200	2,600	3,500	4,000	4,500	Spouse
	7,200	8,700	11,600	13,100	14,700	Total
40	5,200	6,300	8,300	9,300	10,500	You
	2,300	2,800	3,600	4,100	4,600	Spouse
	7,500	9,100	11,900	13,400	15,100	Total
35	5,300	6,400	8,300	9,400	10,600	You
	2,300	2,800	3,700	4,200	4,700	Spouse
	7,600	9,200	12,000	13,600	15,300	Total

APPENDIX IV

Factor 1
Inflation Factor (at 4%)

Years to Retirement	*Factor*	*Years to Retirement*	*Factor*
1	1.04	21	2.28
2	1.08	22	2.37
3	1.12	23	2.46
4	1.17	24	2.56
5	1.22	25	2.67
6	1.27	26	2.77
7	1.32	27	2.88
8	1.37	28	3.00
9	1.42	29	3.12
10	1.48	30	3.24
11	1.54	31	3.37
12	1.60	32	3.51
13	1.67	33	3.65
14	1.73	34	3.79
15	1.80	35	3.95
16	1.87	36	4.10
17	1.95	37	4.27
18	2.03	38	4.44
19	2.11	39	4.62
20	2.19	40	4.80

APPENDIX V

*Factor 2**
Capital Needed at Retirement

Retirement Period	*Rates of Return* 6%	8%	10%	12%
20 Years	16.79	14.31	12.36	10.82
25 Years	20.08	16.49	13.82	11.81
30 Years	23.07	18.30	14.93	12.48
35 Years	25.79	19.79	15.76	12.95
40 Years	28.26	21.03	16.39	13.28

*Factor 3**
Capital Needed to Maintain Pension

Retirement Period	*Rates of Return* 6%	8%	10%	12%
20 Years	4.63	3.70	3.00	2.45
25 Years	6.53	4.96	3.84	3.02
30 Years	8.48	6.14	4.56	3.46
35 Years	10.42	7.21	5.15	3.80
40 Years	12.31	8.15	5.63	4.04

*Assumes a 4% rate of inflation and the annuitization of principal.

APPENDIX VI

Factor 4

Growth Factor to Retirement

Years to Retirement	Growth Factors 6%	8%	10%	12%	Years to Retirement	Growth Factors 6%	8%	10%	12%
1	1.06	1.08	1.10	1.12	21	3.40	5.03	7.40	10.80
2	1.12	1.17	1.21	1.25	22	3.60	5.44	8.14	12.10
3	1.19	1.26	1.33	1.40	23	3.82	5.87	8.95	13.55
4	1.26	1.36	1.46	1.57	24	4.05	6.34	9.85	15.18
5	1.34	1.47	1.61	1.76	25	4.29	6.85	10.83	17.00
6	1.42	1.59	1.77	1.97	26	4.55	7.40	11.92	19.04
7	1.50	1.71	1.95	2.21	27	4.82	8.00	13.11	21.32
8	1.59	1.85	2.14	2.48	28	5.11	8.63	14.42	23.88
9	1.69	2.00	2.36	2.77	29	5.42	9.32	15.86	26.75
10	1.79	2.16	2.59	3.11	30	5.74	10.06	17.45	29.96
11	1.90	2.33	2.85	3.48	31	6.09	10.87	19.19	33.56
12	2.01	2.52	3.14	3.90	32	6.45	11.74	21.11	37.58
13	2.13	2.72	3.45	4.36	33	6.84	12.68	23.22	42.09
14	2.26	2.94	3.80	4.89	34	7.25	13.69	25.55	47.14
15	2.40	3.17	4.18	5.47	35	7.69	14.79	28.10	52.80
16	2.54	3.43	4.59	6.13	36	8.15	15.97	30.91	59.14
17	2.69	3.70	5.05	6.87	37	8.64	17.25	34.00	66.23
18	2.85	4.00	5.56	7.69	38	9.15	18.63	37.40	74.18
19	3.03	4.32	6.12	8.61	39	9.70	20.12	41.14	83.08
20	3.21	4.66	6.73	9.65	40	10.29	21.72	45.26	93.05

APPENDIX VII

Factor 5
Savings Factor to Retirement

Years to Retirement	Savings Factors 6%	8%	10%	12%	Years to Retirement	Savings Factors 6%	8%	10%	12%
1	1.000	1.000	1.000	1.000	21	0.025	0.020	0.016	0.012
2	0.485	0.481	0.476	0.472	22	0.023	0.018	0.014	0.011
3	0.314	0.308	0.302	0.296	23	0.021	0.016	0.013	0.010
4	0.229	0.222	0.215	0.209	24	0.020	0.015	0.011	0.008
5	0.177	0.170	0.164	0.157	25	0.018	0.014	0.010	0.007
6	0.143	0.136	0.130	0.123	26	0.017	0.013	0.009	0.007
7	0.119	0.112	0.105	0.099	27	0.016	0.011	0.008	0.006
8	0.101	0.094	0.087	0.081	28	0.015	0.010	0.007	0.005
9	0.087	0.080	0.074	0.068	29	0.014	0.010	0.007	0.005
10	0.076	0.069	0.063	0.057	30	0.013	0.009	0.006	0.004
11	0.067	0.060	0.054	0.048	31	0.012	0.008	0.005	0.004
12	0.059	0.053	0.047	0.041	32	0.011	0.007	0.005	0.003
13	0.053	0.047	0.041	0.036	33	0.010	0.007	0.004	0.003
14	0.048	0.041	0.036	0.031	34	0.010	0.006	0.004	0.003
15	0.043	0.037	0.031	0.027	35	0.009	0.006	0.004	0.002
16	0.039	0.033	0.028	0.023	36	0.008	0.005	0.003	0.002
17	0.035	0.030	0.025	0.020	37	0.008	0.005	0.003	0.002
18	0.032	0.027	0.022	0.018	38	0.007	0.005	0.003	0.002
19	0.030	0.024	0.020	0.016	39	0.007	0.004	0.002	0.001
20	0.027	0.022	0.017	0.014	40	0.006	0.004	0.002	0.001

APPENDIX VIII

YOUR NET WORTH WORK SHEET

Assets	Fair Market Value
Date:	
CASH AND CASH EQUIVALENTS	
Your checking account(s)	$________
Savings account(s)	________
Cash management account(s)	________
Money-market account(s)	________
Credit union account(s)	________
Certificate(s) of deposit	________
STOCKS AND BONDS	
Stocks	________
Bonds	________
Mutual funds	________
Unit trusts	________
Fixed-income securities	________
Options	________
Futures	________
Commodities	________
REAL-ESTATE INVESTMENTS	
Value of your home	________
Value of your vacation home	________
Rental property	________
Real-estate partnerships	________
Other	________
OTHER INVESTMENTS	
Partnerships:	
Oil and gas	________
Other	________
Ownership interests in businesses	________
COLLECTIBLES	
Gold and silver	________
Art	________
Antiques	________
Other (stamps, etc.)	________
RETIREMENT ASSETS	
IRA	________
Keogh	________
401(k)	________
Company pension plan	________
Profit sharing	________
Savings plan	________

VIII-2

INSURANCE	
Cash value of life insurance	________
Surrender value of annuities	________
PERSONAL PROPERTY	
Automobiles	________
Boats	________
Campers	________
Plane	________
Jewelry	________
Household furnishings	________
Other	________
TOTAL	$________

Liabilities	Value or Balance
Home mortgage	$________
Vacation home mortgage	________
Other real-estate debts	________
Automobile loans	________
Tuition loans	________
Other installment loans	________
Credit cards:	
Bank	________
Retail stores	________
Airline	________
Oil companies	________
Other	________
Credit lines:	
Overdraft line	________
Home equity line	________
Unsecured credit line	________
Income taxes	________
Property taxes	________
Margin loans from brokers	________
Miscellaneous debt	________
TOTAL	$________

Net Worth	
Assets	$________
Less liabilities	$________
NET WORTH	$________

APPENDIX IX

Generally
Recommended
What is the company's A.M. Best rating

FEATURE	GENERALLY RECOMMENDED	PROPOSED POLICY #1	PROPOSED POLICY #2
Monthly premium	It varies		
Daily nursing home benefit	$50.00 & up		
How long until benefits begin?	0 to 180 days		
Max. benefit period - one stay Max. benefit period - all stays	30 months & up 30 months & up		
Does it pay full benefits in a: Skilled Nursing facility? Intermediate facility? Custodial facility?	 Yes Yes Yes		
Is hospitalization not required?	Yes		
Can I enter any level of care?	Yes		
Does it pay for Home Care?	Yes		
Does it pay for Adult Day Care?	Yes		
Are benefits increased for inflation?	Yes		
Does it have waiver of premium?	Yes		
Is it guaranteed renewable?	Yes		
Does the premium stay level?	Yes		
Does it cover mental disorders, e.g., dementia and Alzheimer's	Yes		
Does it cover nervous and muscular disorders?	Yes		
What is the company's A. M. Best rating?	A or A+		

Prepared with contribution from HICAP

APPENDIX X

Social Security Administration
Request for Earnings and Benefit Estimate Statement

To receive a free statement of your earnings covered by Social Security and your estimated future benefits, all you need to do is fill out this form. Please print or type your answers. When you have completed the form, fold it and mail it to us.

1. Name shown on your Social Security card:

   First ______ Middle Initial ______ Last ______

2. Your Social Security number as shown on your card:

   ☐☐☐-☐☐-☐☐☐☐

3. Your date of birth: ______ Month ______ Day ______ Year

4. Other Social Security numbers you may have used:

   ☐☐☐-☐☐-☐☐☐☐

   ☐☐☐-☐☐-☐☐☐☐

5. Your Sex: ☐ Male ☐ Female

6. Other names you have used (including a maiden name):

   ______

   ______

7. Show your actual earnings for last year and your estimated earnings for this year. Include only wages and/or net self-employment income subject to Social Security tax.

   A. Last year's actual earnings:

   $☐☐☐,☐☐☐.[0][0]
   Dollars only

   B. This year's estimated earnings:

   $☐☐☐,☐☐☐.[0][0]
   Dollars only

8. Show the age at which you plan to retire: ______

Form SSA-7004-PC-OP1 (6/88) DESTROY PRIOR EDITIONS

9. Below, show an amount which you think best represents your future average yearly earnings between now and when you plan to retire. The amount should be a yearly average, not your total future lifetime earnings. Only show earnings subject to Social Security tax.

   Most people should enter the same amount as this year's estimated earnings (the amount shown in 7B). The reason for this is that we will show your retirement benefit estimate in today's dollars, but adjusted to account for average wage growth in the national economy.

   However, if you expect to earn significantly more or less in the future than what you currently earn because of promotions, a job change, part-time work, or an absence from the work force, enter the amount in today's dollars that will most closely reflect your future average yearly earnings. Do not add in cost-of-living, performance, or scheduled pay increases or bonuses.

   Your future average yearly earnings:

   $ ☐☐☐,☐☐☐.00
   Dollars only

10. Address where you want us to send the statement:

Name

Street Address (Include Apt. No., P.O. Box, or Rural Route)

City State Zip Code

I am asking for information about my own Social Security record or the record of a person I am authorized to represent. I understand that if I deliberately request information under false pretenses I may be guilty of a federal crime and could be fined and/or imprisoned. I authorize you to send the statement of my earnings and benefit estimates to me or my representative through a contractor.

Please sign your name (Do not print)

Date (Area Code) Daytime Telephone No.

ABOUT THE PRIVACY ACT

Social Security is allowed to collect the facts on this form under Section 205 of the Social Security Act. We need them to quickly identify your record and prepare the earnings statement you asked us for. Giving us these facts is voluntary. However, without them we may not be able to give you an earnings and benefit estimate statement. Neither the Social Security Administration nor its contractor will use the information for any other purpose.

☐ SP

9. Below, show an amount which you think best represents your future average yearly earnings between now and when you plan to retire. The amount should be a yearly average, not your total future lifetime earnings. Only show earnings subject to Social Security tax.

Most people should enter the same amount as this year's estimated earnings (the amount shown in 7B). The reason for this is that we will show your retirement benefit estimate in today's dollars, but adjusted to account for average wage growth in the national economy.

However, if you expect to earn significantly more or less in the future than what you currently earn because of promotions, a job change, part-time work, or an absence from the work force, enter the amount in today's dollars that will most closely reflect your future average yearly earnings. Do not add in cost-of-living, performance, or scheduled pay increases or bonuses.

Your future average yearly earnings:

10. Address where you want us to send the statement.

Name

Street Address (Include Apt. No., P.O. Box, or Rural Route)

City State Zip Code

[illegible]

Please sign your name (Do not print)

[illegible]

Index